Rusk

Stuart Eagles

Second Edition

Published by
The Guild of St George

Published 2016 by the Guild of St George Publications
10 St Oswald's Road, York YO10 4PF

www.guildofstgeorge.org.uk

ISBN 978-0-9932009-6-0

All papers used to print at Reprotech are FSC certified.
We are committed to using sustainable forest print stocks.
All our printing is done on X800, solvent free digital press,

Typeset and printed in England by
Reprotech Studios, 22 Trinity Lane, Micklegate, York YO1 6EL

:

For Pavel

To Robert,
I recall how, after
I gave this lecture,
you approached me to
sign the first edition.
I'm proud to send you
this new version with
my respect, thanks and
friendship to you and
Bunty, ever yours,
Stu.

Acknowledgements

My research has drawn on material held at Yasnaya Polyana (Tolstoy's estate near Tula), the Russian State Library (Rossiiskaya Gosudarstvennaya Biblioteka) in Moscow and the National Library of Russia (Rossiiskaya Natsional'naya Biblioteka) in St Petersburg. I am eternally grateful for the help, advice, encouragement and above all, friendship, of Lidiya Spiridinova, Andrei Kurvanov, Olga Sinitsyna, Tatuana Nikitina, Evgeny Tochilkin, and especially Evgeny Korchagin. In more recent years, my understanding has been enhanced by Natalia Dushkina, and by my friends Pavel Chepyzhov, Aleksandr Osipov, Aleksandr Korchargin and Ksenia Bedunkevich. I would also like to thank Andrew Melling and Alan Wood in whose company my enthusiasm for all things Russian has always thrived. I thank the Guild of St George and its Master, Clive Wilmer, for giving me the opportunity to deliver and publish this lecture. I thank Rebecca Beasley and Matthew Taunton of the Anglo-Russian Research Network for giving me the chance to expand on part of this lecture in the inaugural seminar hosted by that stimulating forum. And I am very grateful to Sara Atwood and Francis O'Gorman for giving me other opportunities to share my exploration of the connections between Ruskin and Russia in print. Finally, thank you to Chris Eagles, Peter Miller and Rachel Dickinson for proofreading this second edition.

Stuart Eagles
(October 2016)

A Note on Translation

I have used the British Standard system for transliteration of Russian, but have omitted diacritics, and I have modernised pre-1918 spellings. Hard signs in names have been removed. Where the accepted rendering of a Russian name in English differs from this system, the conventional spelling has been used, e.g. Maxim not Maksim, Tolstoy not Tolstoi etc, except in quotations which remain faithful to the original at all times. 'Tolstoy' was preferred not only by Aylmer Maude, Tolstoy's friend, biographer and translator, but by Tolstoy himself. Unless otherwise indicated, translations from Russian have been made by me. This second edition was encouraged and facilitated by the indefatigable Peter Miller, Director for Publications of the Guild of St George.

Introduction to the Second Edition

The first edition of this booklet was the basis for The Ruskin Lecture that I gave at the Bar Convent, York, at the AGM of the Guild of St George on 20th November 2010. It has been out-of-print for some time. In re-presenting it here, I have revised the text to take account of studies published in the intervening six years, and I have sought to make a number of minor corrections and clarifications, re-phrasing a number of sentences. I have also added a significant number of illustrations. It has been as enjoyable to revisit this material as it was to do the research for the study in the first place.

Having been fascinated both by Ruskin and Russia for so long, it struck me in 2009 that Tolstoy provided an opportunity to combine the two. It had always been surprising to me—and it remains so—that such little sustained attention had been given by scholars to the relationship between the two men. But since 2010, a number of studies have been published which both build on and considerably add to my work, and they deserve mention here.

Charlotte Alston's *Tolstoy and His Disciples* is a study of influence in much the same vein as my own *After Ruskin* (2011) except that it extends beyond Russia, and Britain, to consider Tolstoyan movements in other parts of Europe.[1] Both the similarities and differences between the networks of discipleship that Ruskin and Tolstoy

[1] See Charlotte Alston, *Tolstoy and His Disciples; The History of a Radical International Movement* (London: I. B. Tauris, 2014) and Stuart Eagles, *After Ruskin: The Social and Political Legacies of a Victorian Prophet, 1870-1920* (Oxford: Oxford University Press, 2011). However, I have since written two short studies of Ruskin's reception in different European countries: see Stuart Eagles, 'Ruskin's "very small circle" of readers in Denmark', *Ruskin Review and Bulletin*, vol. 8, no. 2 (Autumn 2012) pp. 5-13 and 'Ruskin as "world-author": the Netherlands', *Ruskin Review and Bulletin*, vol. 9, no. 2 (Autumn 2013) pp. 4-13. A third is forthcoming: '"How does he think Spaniards will care?": Ruskin's Spanish Readers'.

inspired bear fruitful comparison, and a reading of these studies in tandem is instructive.

Tanya Nikitina's *Neznakomyi Reskin* (*Unfamiliar Ruskin*) is a bold attempt by a Companion of the Guild of St George who is also Senior Researcher at Tolstoy's Yasnaya Polyana, to introduce Ruskin to a wider readership in Russia.[2] It appeared under the imprint of the *Russkii Fond Reskina* (The Russian Ruskin Foundation) of which Nikitina is Executive Director. She explains that the Foundation exists 'to acquaint a Russian audience with the rich spiritual legacy of John Ruskin' (p. 52). It's intention is to encourage the publication of new Russian editions of Ruskin's work, and more broadly to promote British and Russian cultural exchange. This short but elegantly produced introduction to Ruskin consists of chapters on Ruskin's life and heritage, Tolstoy's role in popularising Ruskin in Russia, Tolstoy's favourite Ruskin maxims (67 are quoted), the Guild of St George, Ruskin's home Brantwood, and ending with a timeline of key dates and a useful bibliography.

In 2015 I was delighted to be contacted by Vladislava Polituciaia, a student working under the supervision of Companion Dr Emma Sdegno at the Ca' Foscari University of Venice. I gladly made available to her my research notes on Tolstoy's 'translations' of phrases and short passages by Ruskin. She analysed the English originals and their rendering by Tolstoy into Russian, comparing the two in order to assess both Tolstoy's motivation in publishing them and their (potential) effect on the Russian readers they reached.[3] To my knowledge, such a study has never been attempted before, and it is to be hoped that the research can be expanded and published.

---

[2] See Tatiana Nikitina, *Neznakomyi Reskin* [*Unfamiliar Ruskin*] (Moscow: Molodaya Gvardiya, 2014).
[3] Vladislava Polituciaia, 'John Ruskin and Leo Tolstoy' supervised by Prof. Emma Sdegno (unpublished thesis, Ca' Foscari University of Venice, 2015).

My own essay on 'Political essays' in the *Cambridge Companion to John Ruskin* explored some of the complexities in the multi-layered network of influences between Ruskin, Tolstoy and Gandhi, something which I avoided in the present volume.[4] Not only was Gandhi influenced by both men, but the influence of Ruskin on Tolstoy was evident to Gandhi, too. It is revealing that it was in their philosophies of labour— especially the work of the hand—and their shared belief in the value of a creative life, that their world-views most purposefully intersected and overlapped.

Yet what is said in all these studies, and what is presented here in this second edition of *Ruskin and Tolstoy*, remains a mere introduction to the topic. Although in this lecture I asserted that Tolstoy's reading of Ruskin was deep and wide-ranging, I did not (for lack of space) name the works in which Tolstoy invoked Ruskin in order to add weight to his argument. Such instances occur in essays Tolstoy wrote about writers Timofei Bondarev (1820-1898) and Wilhelm Von Polenz (1861-1903); in *What Is Religion?*, *The Slavery of Our Times*, *The Meaning of the Russian Revolution*, *The Law of Violence and the Law of Love*. In these texts, Tolstoy translated passages from Ruskin's *Fors Clavigera*, *Unto this Last*, *The Stones of Venice* and *The Seven Lamps of Architectur*e. A detailed account and analysis of these references remains to be written.

Nonetheless, studies in recent years have picked up on Ruskin and Tolstoy's relationship: *Persistent Ruskin,* for example, and *The Recovery of Beauty* are two examples of essay collections which suggest a growing appetite to explore connections between the two writers.[5]

---

[4] Stuart Eagles, 'Political legacies' in *The Cambridge Companion to John Ruskin* (Cambridge: Cambridge University Press, 2015) pp. 249-262.

[5] See *Persistent Ruskin: Studies in Influence, Assimilation and Effect*, ed. Keith Hanley and Brian Maidment (London: Routledge, 2013) and *The Recovery of Beauty: Arts, Culture, Medicine* ed. Corinne Saunders, Jane McNaughton and David Fuller (London: Palgrave Macmillan, 2015).

Students, too, have begun to take a keener interest.[6] It is to be hoped that such a scholarly environment will shed new light in the coming years on the subject in hand, providing new insights into two of the greatest writers the world has ever known,

[6] See, for example, references to Ruskin and Russia in Richard Lee Pierre, 'Lyric Petrologies: Languages of Stone in Rilke, Trakl, Mandelstam, Celan and Sachs' (University of Michigan, unpublished doctoral thesis, 2015).

Ruskin and Tolstoy

When Lev Nikolaevich Tolstoy died at the railway station-house in remote Astapovo, exactly one hundred years ago today,[7] he was the most well-known writer in the Russian Empire and already one of the most celebrated authors in the world.[8] The man most fondly remembered now for his remarkable novels, *War and Peace* (1865-69) and *Anna Karenina* (1875-77), had taken flight from his ancestral estate at Yasnaya Polyana (clear glade), 150 miles south of Moscow. On hearing of his death, thousands of peasants and disciples showed their grief in the streets, and student demonstrations soon erupted in the universities. The death of Tolstoy, the scourge of the Tsarist state, the champion of the peasant life, the heretic excommunicated by the Russian Orthodox Church led, in the words of one modern biographer, A. N. Wilson, to:

> one of the most extraordinary demonstrations of public sympathy in the history of the world. No novelist has ever been given such a funeral, but it was not for his novels that they honoured him. It was for the deeds which now seem to us half mad and quixotic; it was for those volumes of his work which most readers now leave unread.[9]

Almost eleven years earlier, John Ruskin, the British critic of art and society who gave practical expression to many of his most profound ideas, had been buried in the quiet churchyard at Coniston which he had designated as his final resting place, a short journey from Brantwood, his Lake District home. Although there was no popular display of grief,

---

[7] This lecture was given on 20th November 2010.

[8] Tolstoy died on 7 November, 1910 according to the Old Style Calendar then in use in Russia, 20 November according to the New Style Calendar now in use in Russia and already in use in the West in 1910.

[9] A. N. Wilson, *Tolstoy* (London: Hamish Hamilton, 1988) (Penguin reprint, 2001) p. 517.

Ruskin's social and political influence was then at its height in Britain. The university settlements were providing an apprenticeship in public service for many of the former Oxford undergraduates who had most admired him, Ruskin societies flourished in major cities, ethical socialists were inspired by his writing to campaign for social reform and political representation for workers, and some of his most dedicated disciples continued the work he had started in his utopian social experiment—the Guild of St George.[10]

It is the later Tolstoy, and the later Ruskin, who together command our attention in this lecture. By the second half of their long lives, Ruskin and Tolstoy had become outspoken, often controversial, relentless and increasingly influential critics of the social and political systems in which they lived. Both were routinely compared to Biblical prophets; for some, they were sages to be revered. Their respective homes became, particularly in the final two decades of their lives, sites of pilgrimage for their disciples and followers. Their collected writings, covering all manner of subjects and filling numerous volumes, represent the highest cultural achievement. In life, in their different ways, they attempted to put their ideas into practice. Neither man escaped censure by critics for the apparent, and sometimes palpable, contradictions that characterised their lives and thought. Yet, always, they lived to strive, and strived to live, in the fullest sense. It can be said of both men, as Aylmer Maude (1858-1938) wrote persuasively of Tolstoy, that they, 'need not fully succeed in [their] quest. [They] may even seem to fail, and yet [their] example may do more to make life worth living than the most brilliant material success could achieve.'[11]

---

[10] For an account of the nature and extent of Ruskin's influence in Britain, see Stuart Eagles, *After Ruskin: The Social and Political Legacies of a Victorian Prophet, 1870–1920* (Oxford: Oxford University Press, 2011).

[11] Aylmer Maude, *The Life of Tolstoy: A Biography* (Ware: Wordsworth, 2008) [*The Life of Tolstoy, First Fifty Years (*1908) and *The Life of Tolstoy:*

Sites of Pilgrimage:
Yasnaya Polyana (*left*) (photo: Alexander Plyakin) and
Brantwood (*right*) (photo: Stuart Eagles).

Much has been written about their philosophical ideals, and their names have often been bracketed together.[12] In 1899, for example, an anonymous writer contributing to *Le Figaro* called Ruskin, 'the Tolstoi of England'.[13] The study, *Prophets of the Nineteenth Century* (1900), by May Alden Ward (1853-1918), though it focused on Carlyle, Ruskin and Tolstoy in discrete chapters, also considered some connections between the three writers in its introductory paragraphs.[14] It is worth quoting at length, in all the glory of its *fin-de-siècle* optimism, not least because

---

Later Years (1910) as revised (Oxford: Oxford University Press, 1930)] p. 887.

[12] Frederic Harrison made the same observation in 1920, see Frederic Harrison, *John Ruskin* (London: Macmillan, 1920) p. 195. J. A. Hobson's study of Ruskin, which was translated into Russian (see below), alludes to Tolstoy at several points, see J. A. Hobson, *John Ruskin, Social Reformer* (London: Nisbet, 1898) pp. 30, 132, 197, 235-6, 237, 259, 236, 237-8, 341.

[13] *Le Figaro* (29 March 1899) qtd in Anon., 'The Figaro and Mr. Ruskin' in *Saint George* [the journal of the Ruskin Society of Birmingham] vol. 2, no. 7 (July 1899) pp. 158-9, specifically p. 159.

[14] May Alden Ward, *Prophets of the Nineteenth Century: Carlyle, Ruskin, Tolstoi* (London: Gay and Bird, 1900).

Ward's study was translated into Russian in the year of its original publication.[15]

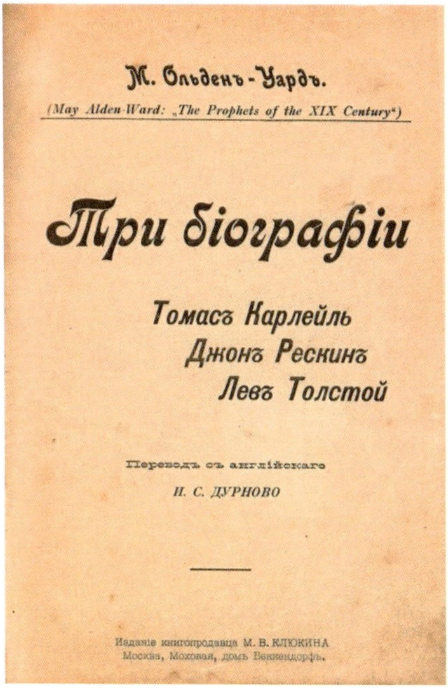

May Alden-Ward], *Tri Biografii: Tomas Karleil', Dzhon Reskin, Lev Tolstoi* (*Three Biographies: Thomas Carlyle, John Ruskin, Lev Tolstoi*), trans. I. S. Durnovo (Moscow: M. V. Klyukin, 1900).

Commending Ruskin for investing his 'private fortune' to advance his ideals, she wrote:

> In this last act we may see a close relation to the teachings and practice of Tolstoi. Though the relation with Tolstoi is less

[15] See M. Ol'den-Uard [also written in English, but incorrectly as May Alden-Ward], *Tri Biografii: Tomas Karleil', Dzhon Reskin, Lev Tolstoi* (*Three Biographies: Thomas Carlyle, John Ruskin, Lev Tolstoi*), trans. I. S. Durnovo (Moscow: M. V. Klyukin, 1900).

> direct [than the relation with Carlyle], and probably not at all organic, it is none the less real; since a spiritual sympathy through the contagion of ideas, may furnish a bond of the most lasting kind. By such a fellowship these three men are absolutely united, — three social reformers working toward the highest ends; and, in spite of local differences, toward almost the same end. With what difficulties they contended and with what struggles of soul they reached their new gospel, of the mission of man to his fellow, the story of each must tell; but there is no longer room to doubt that to each of them it was a gospel, uttered with as complete a sincerity as any that ever came to the heart of man; and as truly has it proved prophetic of the great movement which is now sweeping over the world, proclaiming the coming of sweetness, and joy, and comfort to human life, through the surrender of luxury, greed, and vulgarity. The false gods may fight hard and tarry long, but their disguise is now torn from them. Henceforth they must masquerade in their true character.[16]

It is a powerful point. Common to both men was the desire and attempt to make the invisible visible, to shine a light into dark places, and to expose realities so that everyone could see— and assess — them for what they were.

To Ruskin and Tolstoy, modern industrial capitalism was not merely a threat to nature, but a barrier to the individual's full physical, mental and spiritual self-development. They both perceived the established political philosophy and system of government of the countries in which they lived to be the cause of great misery for the vast majority of the population, and consequently the enemy of their ideals. Both attacked the status quo with crushing ferocity: in Britain, Ruskin wished to revive a society based on the land; in Russia, Tolstoy wished to protect such a society from further incursions by modern industry. The

[16] Ward, *Prophets*, pp. vii-viii.

machine was the secular icon of a degraded humanity, whereas the work of the hands conferred on the worker the opportunity not merely for communion with nature, but with God. Both were deeply spiritual men, many of whose ideas were inspired by Christian ethics, particularly those embodied in the Sermon on the Mount.

It is inevitable that such a simplistic list of points of apparent agreement between Ruskin and Tolstoy threatens to mask the very real differences in the detail of their philosophies. Tolstoy's approval of anarchism and his advocacy of non-violent resistance to evil cannot be easily reconciled with Ruskin's ideas on the need for hierarchical authority, social order and, occasionally, war, to give three examples, and Ruskin's underlying aesthetic vision differs measurably from Tolstoy's asceticism. In his biography of Ruskin, E. T. Cook nevertheless cites the compelling judgement of Ferdinand Brunetière (1849-1906):

> 'However dissimilar the inspiration of Tolstoi and Ruskin,' says one of the greatest of French critics, 'their works nevertheless have certain features in common, and these are their noblest. I would not assert that the authors did not aspire to the glory of writing well; but their first aim and intention was to think rightly, to act effectively, to toil for the perfecting of social life.'[17]

Significantly, each man recognised in the other something of themselves.

Yet, remarkably little has been written about what they knew and thought of each other. The only scholarly essays in the west is that by John Arthos, and those short pieces in Russian by Svetlana Shustova and

---

[17] See E. T. Cook, *The Life of John Ruskin* (2 vols.) (London: George Allen, 1912). For Brunetière's comments, see *Revue des Deux Mondes* (1 December, 1899).

Tatiana Nikitina.[18] Arthos's essay is an exploration of what he sees as Ruskin and Tolstoy's superficially similar yet fundamentally different attitudes to work, and concludes that Tolstoy's doctrines were ultimately self-destructive because they were self-denying, whereas Ruskin's were enabling because they emphasised self-fulfilment through creativity. Shustova and Nikitina provide fascinating but by no means complete accounts of the significance of Tolstoy's role in the dissemination of Ruskin's work in Russia.

This short study will follow in the more practical tradition of these Russian scholars as it attempts to answer some basic questions. How well did Tolstoy know Ruskin's work? What did he read and when? What did he think of what he read? What exactly was Tolstoy's role in promoting Ruskin's ideas to the Russian-speaking world? In turn, what did Ruskin know of and think about Tolstoy? An assessment—at least in basic terms—of what united and divided the two men will be considered in terms of the little-known but significant 'Ruskinian' and 'Tolstoyan', John Coleman Kenworthy (1861-1934) and his utopian colony in Purleigh, Essex.

---

[18] John Arthos, 'Ruskin and Tolstoy: The Dignity of Man,' *Dalhousie Review*, vol. 43, no.1 (Spring 1963) pp. 5-15.; S. R. Shustova, 'K voprosu o roli L. N. Tolstogo v rasporstranenii trudov Dzhona Reskina v Rossii' ('The role of L. N. Tolstoy In disseminating the work of John Ruskin in Russia') in *Problemy fol'kloristiki, istorii, literatury i metodiki ee preobodavaniya* (*Problems of Folklore: The History of Literature and its Teaching*) (Kyibyshev, 1972) pp. 199-201; T. V. Nikitina, 'Dialog drukh kul'tur: Lev Tolstoi i Dzhon Reskin' ('A Dialogue Between Two Cultures: Lev Tolstoy and John Ruskin'), in *Yasnopolyanskii Sbornik* (*Yasnaya Polyana: A Collection)* (Tula: Yasnaya Polyana Publishing House, 2000) pp. 274-278; Tatiana Nikitina, *Neznakomyi Reskin* [*Unfamiliar Ruskin*] (Moscow: Molodaya Gvardiya, 2014).

All Countries and Times

An unusually ill-informed E. T. Cook wrote in volume 38 of the Library Edition of Ruskin's *Works* (published in May 1912): 'I am not aware that Ruskin has been translated into Russian; but Tolstoy's appreciation of him is well known.'[19] However 'well known' Tolstoy's appreciation may have been, the only material Cook and Wedderburn reproduced was limited to two newspaper articles of reported speech, one of which was compared with an account in Aylmer Maude's *Tolstoy and His Problems* (1902).[20] Ruskin had in fact been extensively translated into Russian by this date, and Cook must have been entirely unaware that Tolstoy had given an official seal to his assessment of Ruskin in what has subsequently become a frequently quoted encomium.

Tolstoy wrote of Ruskin (in Russian):

> John Ruskin is one of the most remarkable men not only of England and of our generation, but of all countries and times, He is one of those rare men who think with their hearts ('les grandes pensées viennent du coeur '), and so he thinks and says what he has himself seen and felt, and what everyone will think and say in the future.

This much is familiar in all but one particular, which I will return to. Significantly, however, Tolstoy continued:

> Ruskin is recognized in England as a writer and art-critic, but he is not spoken of as a philosopher, political economist, and

---

[19] John Ruskin, *The Works of John Ruskin*, ed. E. T. Cook and Alexander Wedderburn (39 vols.) (London: George Allen, 1903-12) [hereafter *Works* vol. no. page no.] vol. 38, p. xxii. See also Cook, *Life*, vol. 2, p. 567, where he adds, 'He regarded Ruskin as the greatest Englishman of his time.'
[20] See *Works* 34.729. For Maude's study see Aylmer Maude, *Tolstoy and His Problems* (London: Grant Richards, 1902). The references to Ruskin are on pp. 40-41.

> Christian moralist — just as Matthew Arnold and Henry George are not so spoken of either in England or America. Ruskin's power of thought and expression is, however, such that — in spite of the unanimous opposition he met with, especially among the orthodox economists (even the most radical of them) who cannot but attack him since he destroys their teaching at its very roots — his fame grows and his thoughts penetrate among the public. Epigraphs of striking force taken from his works are to be found more and more often in English books.[21]

This rarely quoted second paragraph of Tolstoy's provides a useful indication of the nature and extent of the Russian's interest in and enthusiasm for the English writer. His appreciation of Ruskin 'as a philosopher, political economist, and Christian moralist' provided the motivation for the active role he played in the dissemination of Ruskin's works and ideas in Russia. Before considering the significance of Tolstoy's assessment of Ruskin, though, it is expedient to explore the context in which it was written and published, not least because the commonly repeated information about it turns out to be misleading.

In none of the studies of Ruskin which quote Tolstoy's praise—at least, in none of those written in English—has the source been (correctly) identified. Moreover, what is quoted is always incomplete, and usually inaccurate (quoted, for example, in the past tense, as if

[21] This is the (faithful) English translation published in L. N. Tolstoy, *Tolstoy Centenary Edition*, ed. Aylmer Maude (21 vols.) (London: Tolstoy Society, 1928-1937), vol. 21 (*Recollections & Essays*) (1937), p. 188. For the original Russian, see L. N. Tolstoy, *Polnoe sobranie sochinenii* (*Complete Collected Works*), ed. Vladimir Chertkov *et al.* (90 vols.) (Moscow, 1928-1958) [Soviet 'Jubilee Edition'], vol. 31, p. 96, with a not altogether accurate explanatory note, p. 286.

Ruskin had already died).[22] This is not surprising, because even Aylmer Maude's translation for volume 21 of the *Tolstoy Centenary Edition* misleadingly gives its year of publication as 1899, and entitles the piece, 'An Introduction to Ruskin's Works'. He also described it inaccurately as 'a note Tolstoy contributed to a booklet of extracts from Ruskin issued by the *Posrednik* firm that did so much to make first-rate literature accessible to the Russian people.'[23]

Tolstoy's comments were in fact published in Russia in 1898 as a preface or foreword (*predislovie*) to a 61-page selection of Ruskin's work published not by *Posrednik* but by the commercially-successful Moscow firm of I. A. Balandin, in their 'Ethical Art Library' series, under the curious title, *Vospitanie. Kniga. Zhenshchina.* (*Education. Book. Woman.*).[24] The title reflects the chapter headings under which Ruskin's writings were presented, with the last two, 'Kniga' (Book) and 'Zhenshchina' (Woman or Womankind) being, respectively, relatively straightforward translations of the lectures 'Of Kings' Treasuries' and 'Of Queens' Gardens' from *Sesame and Lilies* (1865). The first chapter,

---

[22] See, for example, John Ruskin, *The Genius of John Ruskin*, ed. John D. Rosenberg (originally 1963; Boston and London, 1979), p. 11 in which Rosenberg gives the first paragraph only, and in the past tense, providing no source for the quote. Toni Cerutti (ed.), *Ruskin and the Twentieth Century: The Modernity of Ruskinism* (Vercelli, 2000) quoted his source as Rosenberg, and consequently reproduced the same inaccuracy. Most recently, Kevin Jackson quoted the first paragraph only and in the past tense, and implied that this followed other comments that were based on reported speech reproduced from an English newspaper in *Works* 34.729 and no sources are cited, see Kevin Jackson, *The Worlds of John Ruskin* (London: Pallas Athene, 2010) pp. 143-4.

[23] *Tolstoy, Centenary Edition*, vol. 21, p. xxviii.

[24] Dzhon Reskin (John Ruskin), *Vospitanie. Kniga. Zhenshchina.* (*Education. Book. Woman.*) (Moscow: I. A. Balandin, 1898) [preface by Lev Nikolaevich Tolstoi] (reissued, 1901). For Tolstoy's preface, see p. 3. The publication was approved by the censor in St Petersburg on 15 April 1898.

‘Vospitanie’ (translated as ‘Education’, but also meaning ‘Upbringing’ and implying moral instruction) is a more complex mix of passages from letters in *Time and Tide* (1867), including (in order) letters 21, 8, 16 and 25, paragraph 145 from the lecture, ‘The Future of England,’ in *The Crown of Wild Olive* (1866) and ending with most of what remained of Letter 16 in *Time and Tide*, namely, ‘Of Public Education irrespective of Class-distinction. It consists essentially in giving Habits of Mercy, and Habits of Truth (Gentleness and Justice)’.[25] Steeped in the language of moral guidance and social ethics, this Russian anthology represents some of Ruskin’s more didactic writings.

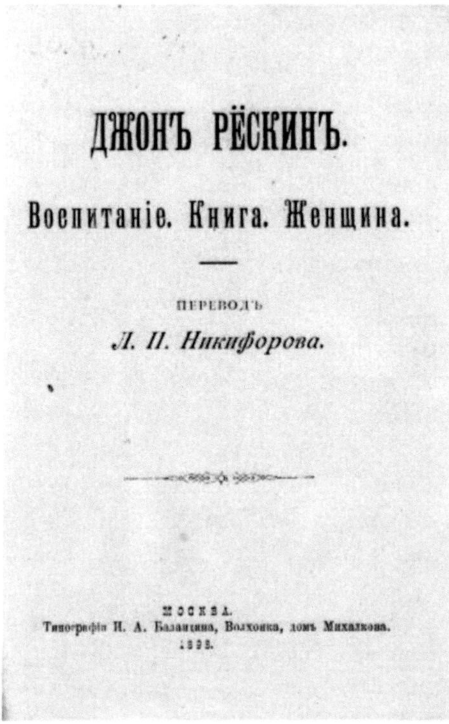

ДЖОНЪ РЁСКИНЪ.

Воспитаніе. Книга. Женщина.

ПЕРЕВОДЪ

Л. П. Никифорова.

МОСКВА.
Типографія И. А. Балашина, Волхонка, домъ Михалкова.
[illegible]

[25] See *Works* 17.425, 17.348, 17.395-6, 17.457-8, 18.502-3 and 17.397-401.

These passages were selected and translated into Russian by Lev Pavlovich Nikiforov (1848-1917). He became Ruskin's principal translator and keenest champion in the Russian Empire, and he was aided considerably in his project to disseminate Ruskin's work and ideas by the sympathetic and enthusiastic support of his influential friend, Tolstoy. Only by looking at Nikiforov's life and work in some detail can the Tolstoyan contribution to the awareness and understanding of Ruskin in Russia be fully appreciated.

Lev Pavlovich Nikiforov

Nikiforov, Posrednik and Ruskin in Russia

Nikiforov, though he became Tolstoy's friend, ought more accurately to be described as one of his disciples, a member of that large group of followers memorably dismissed by Tolstoy's wife, Sofia, as the 'dark ones'.[26] Tolstoy was warm, kind and generous to him, offering him advice, finding him work, and even asking if he could send his children clothes during a time of crisis and hardship for the Nikiforov family.[27] Yet aspects of his life and background made him an unlikely Tolstoyan. He was the son of a wealthy landowner and was educated at both Moscow and St Petersburg Universities.[28] It was at St Petersburg in the late 1860s that he, and the woman he would marry, Ekaterina Zasulich, who had been born into the lesser nobility, mixed with the radical revolutionary, Sergei Nechaev (1847-1882).[29]

Nechaev was forced into exile in Europe where he befriended the revolutionary and theorist of communist anarchism, Mikhail Bakunin (1814-1876), and the two briefly wrote together. Among Nechaev's associates were Nikiforov, Ekaterina Zasulich, and her sister, Vera. In August 1869, Nechaev returned to Russia and set up a terrorist organisation in Moscow called the People's Retribution or the Society of the People's Reprisal (*obschestvo naradnoi raspravy*). A leading member of that organisation, Ivan Ivanovich Ivanov, publicly expressed

---

[26] She specifically describes Nikiforov in this way in her diary entry for 20 January 1899. See Sofia Tolstoy, *The Diaries of Sofia Tolstoy*, ed. Cathy Porter (Richmond: Alma Books, 2009) p. 163.

[27] L. N. Tolstoy, *Tolstoy's Letters*, ed. and trans. R. F. Christian (2 vols.) (London: Athlone, 1978) vol. 2, pp. 464-5.

[28] A brief summary of Nikiforov's background is included in ibid., pp. 463-4.

[29] For more on the Zasulich family, see Alexandra Uspenskaya, 'Vospominanya shestidesyatnitsy' ('Memories of Women of the Sixties'), in *Byloe* (*The Past*), no. 18 (1922), pp. 19-45, see especially pp. 24-8. Uspenskaya was a sister to Vera and Ekaterina.

doubt about Nechaev's methods; such insubordination led to his murder in cold blood. The Third Section, or secret police, vigorously pursued anyone involved with Nechaev, who managed to flee abroad once more. He was eventually caught and tried in 1873, when he was sentenced to twenty years' hard labour in the Peter and Paul Fortress where he died in 1882. It was to that same prison —dubbed the 'Russian Bastille'—that Nikiforov and the Zasulich sisters were eventually taken, after a spell in the notorious Lithuanian Castle. They would be watched by the authorities until the Russian Empire collapsed in 1917.[30]

The notorious Lithuanian Castle prison In St Petersburg.

After their release from prison, Nikikiforov and Ekaterina Zasulich married and lived in Tver, north of Moscow where, during the summer of 1872, police 'uncovered manuscripts and letters implicating

[30] See, for example, S. Nechaev, *A Programme of Revolutionary Action* (1869) and S. Nechaev and M. Bakunin, *Catechism of a Revolutionist* (1869).

Nikiforov in the illegal activities of a group of local seminarians'.[31] Vera Zasulich (1849-1919) was then living with them, and later visited them frequently after the Nikiforovs moved to the village of Penza, southeast of Moscow. Vera Zasulich's biographer, Jay Bergman, explained:

> These visits would be of little significance were it not for the fact that it was in the company of her sister and brother-in-law that Zasulich first read in Gobos [The Voice] in July 1877 of the flogging of Arkhip Bogoliubov in the St Petersburg House of Preliminary Detention.[32]

Vera Zasulich, Nikiforov's sister-in-law.

Morally affronted that a political prisoner should be flogged for failing to doff his cap, in January 1878 Vera walked into the office of the brutal Governor of St Petersburg, General Fyodor Trepov, and shot him with a British bulldog revolver, seriously wounding him., She was

[31] Jay Bergman, *Vera Zasulich: A Biography* (Stanford, Ca.: Stanford University Press, 1983) p. 20.
[32] Ibid., p. 29.

acquitted by the jury in an unprecedented demonstration of sympathy, but was forced to flee to Europe to avoid being re-arrested and re-tried.[33]

Like his sister-in-law, Nikiforov was a Populist, or *Narodnik*, a revolutionary who believed that the true power of Russia was vested in the people, and particularly the *muzhik* (peasant). He opposed the autocratic Tsarist state, and sought to help effect the reform of Russian society along communal and agrarian lines, but it was a revolution that he believed must surge from the mass of agricultural labourers; it would never succeed if imposed from above.

It is not clear how far Lev and Ekaterina Nikiforov were involved in revolutionary activity, but four of their sons perished in the violent struggle against the Tsarist state. Maxim Gorky (1868-1936) immortalised one son, Alexander, in his short chapter, 'The Executioner' in *Fragments From My Diary* (1924).[34] In the revolutionary year of 1905, the 19-year-old Alexander had followed in his aunt Vera's footsteps and shot, at point-blank range, Captain Alexander Vasilevich Greshner, the chief of the secret police in Nizhny Novgorod, killing him instantly. Gorky wrote of Lev Pavlovich (Alexander's father, and Ruskin's translator):

> Lev was a well-known Tolstoyan in his time and a man with a highly dramatic fate: he had four sons who perished one after the other. The oldest, a Social Democrat, worn out by years of jail and exile, died of heart disease; one

[33] The story of Vera Zasulich's attempt to assassinate Trepov was the inspiration for Oscar Wilde's melodrama, *Vera, or the Nihilists* (1883).
[34] The degree of Nikiforov's sacrifice for revolutionary activity was recognised by the Socialist Revolutionary Party on his death in 1917, with the publication of *Pamyati L'va Pavlovicha Nikiforova: Materialy dla biografii* (*In Memory of Lev Pavlovich Nikiforov: Biographical Materials*) (Moscow: Land and Freedom, 1917).

doused himself with kerosene and burned himself to death; one poisoned himself; and the youngest, Sasha, was hanged for murdering Greshner.[35]

Having read Tolstoy, and put some of his ideas into practice on his ancestral estate in Penza, Nikiforov first met his master in 1884 after he was granted permission to live in Moscow, his exile having finally ended.[36] The most significant outcome of the friendship that developed between the two men was the opportunity it afforded Nikiforov to help foment a peasant revolution through the promotion of educational literature designed to enrich cultural knowledge and elevate popular taste by combatting the ubiquitous *lubochnaya kartinka* (cheap popular print).

Nikiforov played a key role as a translator in the Tolstoyan project to create a Peasants' Library to promote popular education. He believed that only an educated peasantry would and could demand change. *Posrednik* (Intermediary or Mediator) was a publishing firm established to make the best of the world's literature available as cheaply as possible. Established by Tolstoy's friend and collaborator, Vladimir Chertkov (1854-1936), its purpose was to provide, Chertkov wrote, 'good spiritual food for the hearts and minds of our readers'.[37] Its first publisher, Ivan Sytin (1851-1934), who was born into the peasantry, had made his fortune in publishing. He described the missionary objectives of the

---

[35] Maxim Gorky, *Gorky's Tolstoy & Other Reminiscences*, ed. and trans. Donald Fanger (New Haven and London: Yale University Press, 2008) pp. 98-9. For corroboration and further details, see G. H. Perris, *Russia in Revolution* (2nd. edn.) (London: Chapman and Hall, 1905) pp. 117, 279-80.
[36] Anon., 'Russia' in *The Times* (30 September 1881) referred to 'the exiles Nikiforoff and the famous Vera Zassulitch' (p. 5).
[37] Qtd in Robert Otto, *Publishing for the People (The Firm Posrednik, 1885-1905)* (New York and London: Garland Publishing Inc., 1987) p. 134. Also, see Alexander Fodor, *A Quest for a Non-Violent Russia, The Partnership of Leo Tolstoy and Vladimir Chertkov* (London: University Press of America, 1989).

endeavour most effectively when he wrote that, 'This was not simple work but holy service.'[38] Reflecting Tolstoy's views, opinions and literary tastes, *Posrednik* published 600 of the world's finest books between 1885 and 1906 mainly novels and short stories, short series on the lives and teachings of selected saints, historical figures, and 'wise men'. From 1888, they also published tracts opposing the consumption of alcohol and tobacco smoking.

It was as a result of Tolstoy's sympathetic appreciation of Ruskin, and Nikiforov's enthusiasm for the Englishman's work and ideas, that *Posrednik* published seven Ruskin volumes, which represents about 1% of the firm's output up to 1904. The earliest of these publications, a 47-page biography of Ruskin, written by Nikiforov, appeared in 1896 in the 'Wise Men' series (issue 57) under the title, *Dzhon Rëskin. Ego zhizn', idei i deyatel'nost', Biograficheskii ocherk* (*John Ruskin. His Life, Ideas and Work, A Biographical Sketch*) [s portretom Reskina (with a portrait of Ruskin)].[39]

It was as a preface to this publication for the benefit of *Posrednik* readers, that Tolstoy's two-paragraph celebration of Ruskin had been written. The censor apparently would not approve it, however, meaning that Nikiforov's biography the text of which was passed by the censor on 10 January 1895, was delayed, eventually being published in 1896 without Tolstoy's foreword.[40] It is worth looking at this volume in some detail, not only for what it tells us about how Ruskin was introduced to what we might term the workmen and labourers of Imperial Russia, but

---

[38] For general information on Sytin's publishing ventures, see Charles A. Ruud, *Russian Entrepreneur: Publisher Ivan Sytin of Moscow (1851-1934)* (Montreal & Kingston, McGill-Queen's University Press, 1990).
[39] L. P. Nikiforov, *Dzhon Rëskin. Ego zhizn', idei i deyatel'nost', Biograficheskii ocherk* (*John Ruskin. His Life, Ideas and Work (A Biographical Sketch)*) (Moscow: Posrednik, 1896).
[40] See Shustova, 'Reskina v Rossii,' p. 199.

also for what it can tell us about Nikiforov's understanding of Ruskin, and the nature of his interest in him. We can be confident that Tolstoy would have been familiar with its contents. Close scrutiny is all the more worthwhile because the biography has never been translated into English, and it is doubtful that it has ever been written about at all outside Russia before now.

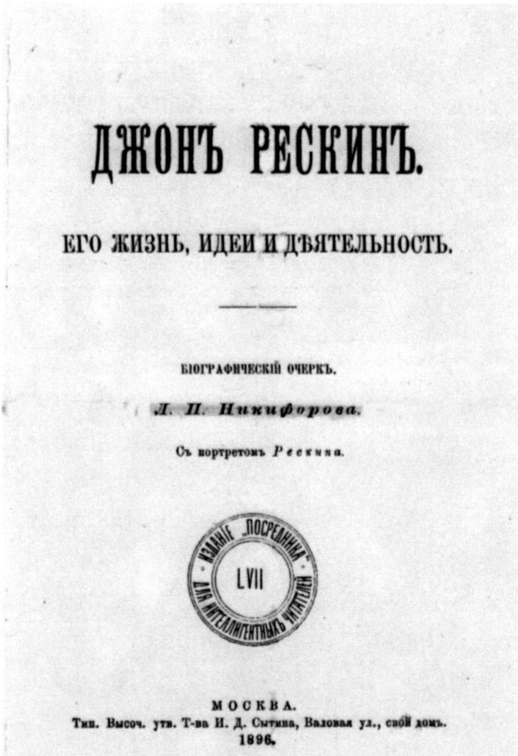

ДЖОНЪ РЕСКИНЪ.

ЕГО ЖИЗНЬ, ИДЕИ И ДѢЯТЕЛЬНОСТЬ.

БІОГРАФИЧЕСКІЙ ОЧЕРКЪ.

Л. П. Никифорова.

Съ портретомъ *Рескина.*

ИЗДАНІЕ „ПОСРЕДНИКА" ДЛЯ ИНТЕЛЛИГЕНТНЫХЪ ЧИТАТЕЛЕЙ

LVII

МОСКВА.
Тип. Высоч. утв. Т-ва И. Д. Сытина, Валовая ул., свой домъ.
1896.

At approximately 10,000 words it is a short introduction, plainly and clearly written, and therefore appropriate for its target readership. Nikiforov emerges as sensitive, knowledgeable and enthusiastic. The volume's emphasis reflected Tolstoy's judgement that Ruskin should be regarded as 'a philosopher, political economist, and Christian moralist'.

Ruskin's aesthetic views are briefly summarised, but the focus then shifts to Ruskin as a teacher in Oxford and his 'many-sided activity': the packed lecture halls, the Hinksey road, the involvement of Arnold Toynbee and the praise of Prince Leopold are all invoked as examples of Ruskin's 'tremendous moral influence'.[41] Casting Ruskin as a social reformer, Nikiforov derived from him three main causes of social evil: the general lack of self-knowledge; the unsuitability of the environments in which the people were forced to live; and the collective failure purposefully to challenge the existing order. This perhaps better reflected Nikiforov's own political priorities than Ruskin's, but he demonstrated that he was widely read in Ruskin: he quotes from the 1871 preface to *Sesame and Lilies*, from *The Stones of Venice* (1851-3), *A Joy For Ever* (1857), *Unto this Last* (1860, 1862) and from Marshall Mather's biography of 1883, none of which were then available to him in Russian.[42]

Nikiforov took some care to describe Ruskin's view of political economy. Unsurprisingly, given both his own politics and his intended readership, his emphasis was on Ruskin's exposure of the evils of modern industrial capitalists and the wrongheadedness of economic theorists in caring merely about material production and not at all for the spiritual development of the workers. Nikiforov underlined Ruskin's message that we must all take responsibility for our condition in life, doing what we can to help those least capable of helping themselves. We must recognise that it is through the activity of work and what we do to earn a living that we achieve true happiness, because that is how we fulfil our spiritual

[41] Nikiforov, *Dzhon Reskin*, pp. 15, 16. On Hinksey, it is worth remembering E. T. Cook's comment that 'Ruskin's road-digging experiment gave a real stimulus to "the gospel of labour," of the same kind as the later and independent teaching of Count Tolstoi.' See Cook, *Life*, vol. 2, p. 189.
[42] J. Marshall Mather, *Life and Teaching of John Ruskin* (Manchester, 1883). This biography was never translated into Russian.

needs: 'the real economy should strive to develop that most precious of all things, the people'.[43]

The study then recounts details of Ruskin's own practical attempts at reform: 'he is not satisfied with a statement of truth, and tries to translate it and apply it'.[44] This was clearly important to Nikiforov, as a letter from Tolstoy written around the time that he was writing this biography indicates:

> I fully understand that you won't like the opinion that a writer needs to be judged by his writings, and not by what he does. This opinion offends me too. But as I told you at the time, my only comment is that writing is the writer's business, as Pushkin aptly said, i.e. if a good blacksmith or worker drinks a lot, I ought to take his work into account and not compare him to an idle drunkard... As for a man needing to strive with all his might to do and perform what he says, this goes without saying, since this is the basis of human life. I would even say that if a man doesn't strive with all his might to do what he says, he will never be good at saying what ought to be done, he will never infect others.[45]

Nikiforov was apparently not persuaded on the first point. He included as examples of Ruskin's practical 'translation' of his ideas into practice, the May Queen festivals at Whitelands College. But it was the Guild of St George that provided the exemplary case. Nikiforov quoted from the Master's Report (1882) as well as the *General Statement* of the same year. Nikiforov refers to projects in Totley and Worcestershire, the Isle

---

[43] Nikiforov, *Dzhon Reskin*, p. 29.
[44] Ibid., p. 36.
[45] Tolstoy to Nikiforov (3 November 1893), qtd in Tolstoy, *Letters*, ed. and trans. R. F. Christian, vol. 2, p. 498.

of Man, the Langdale Linen Industry and Thomson's co-operative woollen mill in Huddersfield (although here he made an uncharacteristic error and called him 'Dzhon Tomson' (John Thomson) instead of George). He commends Ruskin's practical experiments despite and perhapse partly because of the criticism that they had met with in England, opposition to Ruskin's endeavours that he noted with some degree of exasperation.[46]

He concludes with what he calls 'a brief overview of [Ruskin's] literary work' referring to 'more than forty volumes' and specifying *Modern Painters* (1843-60), *The Seven Lamps of Architecture* (1849), *The Stones of Venice*, and finally *Fors Clavigera* (1871-84) which he describes as addressing 'all kinds of public and social issues, with a view to the spiritual development of the English working people'.[47] Nikiforov's final words reflect the enthusiasm with which he wished his readers to join him in celebrating Ruskin. 'Ruskin … has the property of all the great writers: one who fully immerses the soul in their work and so could not help attracting the reader …' Nikiforov was, without doubt, one of Ruskin's most ardent and significant admirers, appealing to a readership that Ruskin surely never dreamed he would reach:

> If this poor and brief essay has prompted a desire in its readers to take a closer look at the activities and works of this figure who shines so brightly, I will consider that my goal has been achieved, and that my work is not in vain.[48]

It is not possible to know how many people read this account, or even how many people purchased it, let alone to discover their social status, political opinion or what they thought of the booklet. The 1897 census revealed that despite the considerable expansion of mass

---

[46] For the Thomson error, see Nikiforov, *Dzhon Reskin*, p. 43.
[47] Ibid., p. 45.
[48] Ibid., pp. 46-7.

education, only 29.3% of Russian males and 13.1% of Russian females were literate, and most of those who could read lived in the cities. As late as 1913 the level of literacy in towns was estimated at a mere 45%, with only 17% of the population in rural areas able to read—an overall literacy in the population of perhaps 30%.[49] Robert Otto's study of the *Posrednik* venture concluded that, regardless, 'the entire cause of publishing for the people had always been a cause that had the intelligentsia as its object just as much as, if not more than, the people' and yet, as he conceded, *Posrednik* 'stands out as a significant landmark in Russia's cultural and social history'. [50]

Nikiforov's claim that he was one of Ruskin's 'major admirers' was no idle boast. Before the publication of his biography of Ruskin, he translated *The King of the Golden River* (1851), a title that was first published in 1894 and republished *by Posrednik* in 1903 and again in 1910.[51] He had been reading Ruskin since at least 1890, when Tolstoy lent him two unidentified volumes from his own library.[52] Nikiforov went on to select and translate for *Posrednik* three short volumes of passages from Ruskin under the title *Izbranne Mysli Dzhona Reskina* (*The Selected*

---

[49] See Catriona Kelly and David Shepherd (ed.), *Constructing Russian Culture in the Age of Revolution, 1881-1940* (Oxford: Oxford University Press, 1998) p. 16.

[50] Otto, pp. 229, 127.

[51] Dzhon Reskin (John Ruskin), *Tsar' Zolotoi Reki ili "Chernye Brat'ya": (Shtiriisk. Legenda Dzhona Reskina)* (*The King of the Golden River, or "The Black Brothers" (Styrian. Legend by John Ruskin)*) (Moscow: P. K. Pryanishnikov, 1894). Nikiforov's version of this fairy tale, globally the most translated of all Ruskin's works, was reissued at least four times, first in 1901 (by Vil'de), then in 1903 (by *Posrednik* publisher, I. D. Sytin), then in 1910 (again under the *Posrednik* imprint) and in 1912 (by A. F. Sukhov in St Petersburg). See also John Ruskin, *The King of the Golden River or The Black Brothers*, ed. James S. Dearden (Freshwater, Isle of Wight: Coach House Publication, 1999) especially pp. 67-112.

[52] See Tolstoy, *Letters*, ed. and trans. R. F. Christian, vol. 2, p. 464.

Thoughts of John Ruskin) published between 1899 and 1904, for the 'Remarkable Thinkers of the Ancient and Modern World' series 'For Intelligent Readers'.[53] These were anthologies which Tolstoy frequently consulted.[54]

Nikiforov's *Selections from Ruskin* (3 vols.) (1899-1904) published by Tolstoy's publishing company, *Posrednik*.

The last Ruskin translation Nikiforov completed for *Posrednik* (though not the last work they published) appeared in 1903: his 159-page translation of Henrietta Bruhnès's *Ruskin et la Bible* (1901).[55] It is highly

---

[53] Dzhon Reskin (John Ruskin), *Izbranye Mysli Dzhona Reskina* (*The Selected Thoughts of John Ruskin*) (3 vols.) (Moscow: Posrednik, 1899-1904) (reissued: Moscow: Vil'de, 1912). Vol. 1 (1899) 32pp., vol. 2 (1902) 47pp., vol. 3 (1904) 42pp.

[54] See, for example, L. N. Tolstoy, *Tolstoy's Diaries*, ed. and trans. R. F. Christian (2 vols.) (London: Athlone, 1985) (18 August 1901 and 2 January 1902) vol. 2, pp. 496, 499.

[55] G. I. Brunges (H. I. Bruhnès), *Reskin i Bibliya: k istorii odnoi mysli* (*Ruskin and the Bible: A History of His Thought*) trans. L. P. Nikiforov [i.e, Henrietta Bruhnès, *Ruskin et la Bible: pour servir a l'histoire d'une pensées* (Paris: Perrin, 1901)].

probable that Tolstoy personally commissioned this work, because the original book profoundly interested and impressed him, earning it his high praise. In a letter to Aylmer Maude, he wrote, 'I recently read an excellent book about him: *Ruskin et la Bible*, by Hugues [Brunhes], I think.'[56] On a visit to Yasnaya Polyana with two American friends in 1903, Sydney Carlyle Cockerell (1867-1962)—at one time secretary to William Morris, and later Director of the Fitzwilliam Museum, Cambridge—reported that Tolstoy asked the group he was with, 'Had we seen a book called *Ruskin et la Bible*? No? you must get it. There was a man who read his Bible, and to some purpose. He was a very great man.'[57]

An earlier translation of Nikiforov's was the seventh and final Ruskin work to be published by *Posrednik*. *Poslednemu, chto i pervomu* [i.e *Unto this Last*] which appeared in 1906 (*Posrednik*'s 651st publication) and was reprinted in 1910.[58] The original translation had been given the subtitle *chetyre ocherka osnov printsipov politecheskoi ékonomii* (*four essays on the principles of political economy*), but this was changed by *Posrednik*'s editors to the more worker-friendly, *ocherki po rabochemu voprosu* (*essays on the labour question*).

---

[56] L. N. Tolstoy to Aylmer Maude (28? July 1901), qtd in Tolstoy, *Letters*, ed. and trans. R. F. Christian, vol. 2, p. 600.
[57] Viola Meynell (ed.), *Friends of a Lifetime: Letters to Sydney Carlyle Cockerell* (London: Jonathan Cape, 1940) p. 82.
[58] Dzhon Reskin (John Ruskin), *Poslednemu, chto i pervomu* (*Unto this Last* [literally, *The Latter, as the First*]) (Moscow: I. A. Balandin, 1900) (reissued: 1, Moscow: Posrednik, 1906; 2, Moscow: Posrednik, 1910).

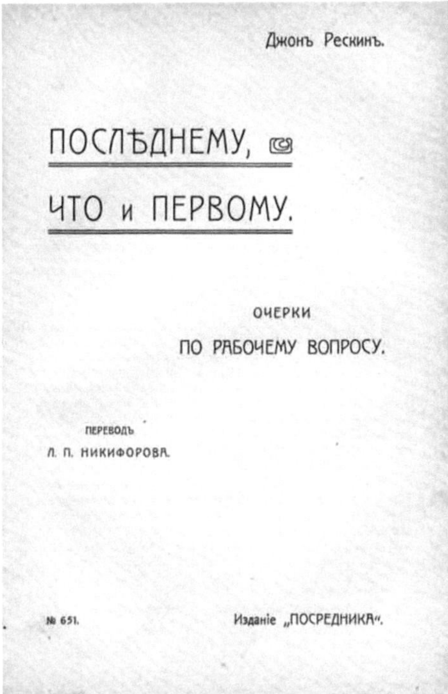

Posrednik's edition of Nikiforov's translation of *Unto this Last.*

Nikiforov's enthusiasm for Ruskin went far beyond his work for *Posrednik*, however. In 1899, his translation of J. A. Hobson's *John Ruskin, Social Reformer* (1898) was published, followed in 1900 by his translation of Robert de la Sizeranne's *Ruskin et la religion de la beauté* (1897).[59]

---

59 See Dzhon Gobson (John Hobson), *Dzhon Rëskin, kak sotsial'nyi reformator* (*John Ruskin as a Social Reformer*) (Moscow: K. T. Soldatenkov, 1899) [i.e. J. A. Hobson, *John Ruskin, Social Reformer* (London: Nisbet, 1898)] and Robert Sizerann (Robert de la Sizeranne), *Reskin i religiya krasoty* (*Ruskin and the Religion of Beauty*) (Moscow: Magazina "Knizhnoe Delo" and I. A. Balandin, 1900) (reissued, Moscow: Komkniga, 2007) [i.e.

A collaboration between Nikiforov, the publisher I. A. Balandin and other firms resulted in the publication of a series of ten of Ruskin's works under the title *Sobranie Sochinenii Dzhona Reskina* (*The Collected Works of John Ruskin*) (1900-4), all inexpensive paperback editions. This was followed by a second 'series' consisting of one much longer and more expensive hardback volume (1905). The first series comprised *Sesame and Lilies*, *Letters and Advice to Women and Young Girls* (based on the 1879 American selection), *Unto this Last* (1862) (noted above), *Lectures on Art* (1870), *The Crown of Wild Olive*, *Ethics of the Dust* (1866), *Frondes Agrestes* (1874), *A Joy For Ever* (1857), *The Laws of Fesole* (1877-8) and *The Eagle's Nest* (1872). The more expensive volume from the second 'series' was a 363-page selection from *Fors Clavigera* (1871-84)—appropriately inaccessible and scarce in Russia given the difficulty many people had in acquiring Ruskin's original monthly instalments in England [60]

As a collection of Ruskin's work, it is not unrepresentative, with a wide selection from his catholic range, but the emphasis was clearly on Ruskin's social, economic and political philosophy, reflecting the interests and prioties not only of Nikiforov but also of his master, Tolstoy. Nikiforov was responsible for translating a total of three books about Ruskin, four selections from Ruskin, and twelve books by Ruskin, as well as writing his own short biography of him. These twenty volumes

---

Robert de la Sizeranne, *Ruskin et la religion de la beauté* (Paris, Hachette, 1897)].

[60] For full details of Dzhon Reskin (John Ruskin), *Sobranie Sochinenii Dzhona Reskina* (*The Collected Works of John Ruskin*) trans. L. P. Nikiforov, (series 1, 10 vols; series 2, 1 vol.) (1900-1905), see the bibliography, section (1) (a).

represent about half of the Ruskin-related titles published in pre-revolutionary Russia.[61]

Tolstoy on Ruskin

Tolstoy's enthusiasm for Ruskin was not expressed only vicariously. Tolstoy used his influence to ensure that *Posrednik* published Nikiforov's translations, but he also engaged directly with Ruskin's work himself, as the evidence of his diaries, correspondence and witnesses (principally visitors to him at Yasnaya Polyana) makes clear.

Ruskin and Tolstoy never met, although Tolstoy did visit England, after going to Germany and France, in 1860-61, when he was studying educational methods as part of his project to run a school on his estate for the children of his serfs. Sydney Cockerell regretted the fact that they never made direct contact with each other, writing that, 'The two men ought to have met. They had very much in common besides a

[61] This is not to suggest that Nikiforov's writing was confined to Ruskin. He translated Carlyle's chapter 'The Sphinx' from *Past and Present* for I. A. Balandin (1900), *Selected Thoughts of Giuseppe Mazzini* for P*osrednik* (1905), a speech by Robespierre and volumes by Henry George, the French geographer and anarchist Élisée Reclus, he wrote about Dostoevsky, and he compiled two volumes of Tolstoy's work, one of which, *Aphorisms and Ideas*, was published by *Posrednik* (1912), and he wrote a short biography of his master, too. Some of Nikiforov's observations were published as *Svedeniya o zemle v Rossii* (*Information on the Ground in Russia*) (1906), but the last ten years of Nikiforov's life appear to have been largely unproductive, undermined by the personal sacrifices his family had made in the revolutionary cause. For a more complete account of the publishing history of Ruskin in Russia, see Stuart Eagles, '"For Fear of Bears": Ruskin in Russia' in *Nineteenth-Century Prose* ed. Sara Atwood, vol. 38, no. 2 (Fall 2011) pp. 157-194.

love of Dickens, a distrust of science, and a readiness to accept the literal word of the Gospel.'[62]

A formidably accomplished linguist who read, wrote and spoke English fluently, Tolstoy read Ruskin—and Sterne, Dickens, Eliot and Arnold among others—in the original, largely eschewing the problem of 'reception' attending authors who appear 'whole' in translation. Because translated works tended to appear out of (their original) sequence and were published in quick succession, little or nothing was generally understood about the order in which the books had originally been written and published. Readers in the 'receiver-culture' rarely had a reliable sense of an author's development over time, and the historical context in which their works had appeared. It was a difficulty which attended Tolstoy in English translation.[63] For most readers in Russia, who relied on the Russian translations of Ruskin, the same problem applied.

Tolstoy was reading Ruskin seriously in the 1880s, but an initially cool response grew gradually warmer until eventually he became an admirer. This development can be traced in Tolstoy's diaries. He noted in January 1889, 'Read Ruskin. Nothing special.'[64] Two months later, he wrote:

> Read Ruskin all morning. Good on art. Science, he says, knows; art creates. Science asserts the fact; art the manifestations. It's the other way round. Art has to do with facts, science with external laws. Art says: the sun, light,

---

[62] See Meynell (ed.), *Friends*, p. 82.

[63] W. Gareth Jones has written that Tolstoy 'had reached England all of a piece, novelist, thinker and social commentator combined', see W. Gareth Jones, 'Introduction' in *idem* (ed.), *Tolstoi and Britain* (Oxford: Berg, 1995) p. 10.

[64] Tolstoy, *Diaries*, ed. and trans. R. F. Christian (5 January 1889) vol. 1, p. 236.

> warmth, light; science says the sun is 111 times bigger than the earth ...[65]

By 1895, he was writing that he had 'read Ruskin's splendid Birthday Book and made notes in it.'[66] In 1900 he was able to record, 'Read George Eliot and Ruskin, and appreciated them very much.'[67]

Tolstoy owned several volumes of Ruskin that survive in his library today. The catalogue of his extant collection of foreign-language books at Yasnaya Polyana lists only six Ruskin books: an American edition of *The King of the Golden River*, George Allen editions of *The Nature of Gothic* (published in 1892, but printed by the Kelmscott Press, with William Morris's introduction), the three volumes of *Praeterita*, two volumes of *Selections from the Writings of John Ruskin* (1901) and *Unto this Last* (4th edn, 1884).[68] Some of these have unopened pages, but *Unto this Last* looks thoroughly read and contains at least 29 underlinings in violet-coloured pencil.[69] He also owned the second edition of

---

[65] Ibid. (11 March 1889) vol. 1, p. 243.

[66] Ibid. (6 April 1895) vol. 2, p. 404. This must be John Ruskin, *The Ruskin Birthday Book: A Selection of Thoughts, Mottoes, and Aphorisms* ed. Maud Bateman and Grace Allen (Orpington: George Allen, 1883) although Christian apparently misidentifies the work. For an analysis of such selections, see Christina Rieger, '"Sweet Order and Arrangement": Victorian Women Edit John Ruskin' *in Journal of Victorian Culture,* vol. 6, no. 2 (Autumn 2001) pp. 231-249.

[67] Tolstoy, *Diaries*, ed. and trans. R. F. Christian (21 August 1900) vol. 2, p. 480.

[68] See V. Bulgakov, N. N. Gusev and E. A. Novikova (eds), *Biblioteka L'va Nikolaevicha Tolstogo v Yasnoj Polyan*e (Catalogue of Foreign Language Books in Tolstoy's Library) (2 vols.) (Moscow, 2000) items 2820-2824.

[69] Many pages of *The King of the Golden River* and *Praeterita* and pp. 26-31 of *The Nature of Gothic* remain unopened, but both volumes of *Selections* appear to have been read in their entirety.

Collingwood's Life (1900), although 44 pages are unopened.[70] Tolstoy's copies of Ruskin in Russian included Nikiforov's *Unto this Last* (the original and the *Posrednik* editions) and a heavily underlined edition of Nikiforov's *Selected Thoughts of John Ruskin,* as well as *Lectures on Art*, and Olga Solov'ëva's wide-ranging selection, *Isskusstvo i deistvitel'nost': izbrannye stranitsy* (Art and Reality: Selected Passages) (1900).[71]

Although it is only possible to speculate, one explanation for this relatively modest number of apparently under-used Ruskin books known definitely to have been in Tolstoy's possession is contained in a letter Tolstoy wrote to Nikiforov in which he told his disciple not to replace two Ruskin volumes he had loaned him that had perished in a fire that consumed Nikiforov's home in July 1890.[72] It is conceivable that Tolstoy loaned out other Ruskin books and that he did not always have them returned. It should also be remembered that Yasnaya Polyana suffered considerable losses and damage when German troops occupied the estate in 1941.

Notwithstanding, it can be said with confidence that Tolstoy knew Ruskin's work intimately, and the claim that, 'He had read most of [Ruskin's] books, beginning with *Unto this Last*' should be believed.[73]

---

[70] W. G. Collingwood, *The Life of John Ruskin* (2nd edn) (London: Methuen and Co., 1900) [item 651 in the catalogue].

[71] See Olga Solov'eva, *Isskusstvo i deistvitel'nost': izbrannye stranitsy* (*Art and Reality: Selected Passages*) (Moscow: 1900). Two editions appeared almost simultaneously, one by I. N. Kushnerev and the other by A. I. Mamontov. It is not clear which printing Tolstoy owned. See Nikitina, 'Dialog', p. 275. Some Ruskin volumes, although it is not possible to identify which ones, were sent to Tolstoy by Sydney Cockerell, see Tolstoy to Cockerell (13 May 1904) qtd Meynell (ed.), *Friends*, p. 86.

[72] Tolstoy to Nikiforov (21-22 July 1890) qtd in Tolstoy, *Letters*, ed. and trans. R. F. Christian, vol. 2, p. 464.

[73] See Meynell (ed.), Friends, p. 82 and also qtd in *Works* 34.729.

The passage Cook and Wedderburn quoted from the *Pall Mall Gazette* in 1892, published when Cook was editor of that journal, demonstrates that Tolstoy's views were established long before the publication of his preface of praise in 1898:

> Ruskin he thought one of the greatest men of the age. 'When Ruskin,' he said, 'began to write on philosophy and on morality, he was ignored by everybody, especially by the English press, which has a peculiar way of ignoring anybody it does not like. I am not astonished that people speak so little of Ruskin in comparison with Gladstone. When the latter makes a speech, the papers are loud with their praises, but when Ruskin, whom I believe to be a greater man, talks, they say nothing.' [74]

This closely anticipates what Tolstoy's later encomium, and the positive comparison with Gladstone was repeated by Aylmer Maude and John Kenworthy.[75]

Cook and Wedderburn's other source, an uncredited account from the *Daily Chronicle*, in fact came from Cockerell, who told his friend, the poet and essayist Wilfrid Scawen Blunt (1840-1922), 'We talked much of Ruskin and Morris'.[76] Cockerell's contemporary notes, reproduced in the first volume of his published correspondence, provide further evidence of Tolstoy's good opinion of Ruskin. Tolstoy had said, 'I like his face ... I have seen two portraits, front face and profile, both after he

---

[74] *Pall Mall Gazette* (26 May 1892) qtd *Works* 34.729.
[75] See Maude, *Problems*, p. 40. See Anon., 'Ruskin and Reform' in *Saint George*, vol. 3, no. 12 (October 1900) pp. 219-222, reproducing a letter from John Kenworthy to the *Daily News* (4 August 1900) specifically p. 220.
[76] Wilfrid Scawen Blunt, *Cockerell: Sydney Carlyle Cockerell, Friend of Ruskin and William Morris and Director of the Fitzwilliam Museum, Cambridge* (London: Hamish Hamilton, 1964) p. 106.

had grown a beard. He was like a Russian peasant.' [77] This is high praise from Tolstoy, who revered the peasantry, but it prompted John Arthos in his essay on the two men to write, somewhat exaggeratedly, 'One may doubt how well Tolstoy understood Ruskin':

> If he meant passion and intensity and endurance, of course —but he meant more than that, he meant that peasants are like Ruskin, and nothing could be much farther from the truth than that.[78]

Taking the comment quite literally at *fac*e value (as well he might), Cockerell observed that Tolstoy's remark, 'is still more true of Tolstoy himself, whose type of face, with less force and less keenness in the eye but the same features, may be seen again and again in the streets of Tula and Moscow.'[79] He went on, 'In manner and speech he is very gentle, ready to listen as well as to talk, more like Ruskin in this respect than anyone else I could recall.'[80]

In a passage not reproduced by Cook and Wedderburn, Cockerell wrote that:

> Many readers of *What is Art?* have been surprised by [Tolstoy] making no reference to Ruskin or William Morris, although various unimportant English writers are quoted, as well as scientists like Darwin, Herbert Spencer and Grant Allen, who could not be expected to speak on such a subject with knowledge and authority. One of us ventured to express this.[81]

---

[77] Meynell (ed), *Friends*, p. 82.
[78] Arthos, 'Ruskin and Tolstoy', p. 10.
[79] Meynell (ed.), *Friends*, p. 82.
[80] Ibid.
[81] Ibid., p. 81.

Tolstoy replied, in the words of the scholar, R. F. Christian, 'not altogether logically':[82]

> Is this so? ... perhaps you are right. I am in the habit of dividing my fellow men into two classes, the foolish and the clever (wise?) and I put all scientists into the former class.[83]

Aylmer Maude asked him the same question, and published his translation of Tolstoy's letter of response, but Christian's is more accurate:[84] 'Ruskin ascribed too much importance to beauty in art and, although many of the ideas in his writings were profound, they were not connected by a central, unifying idea'.[85] To extend this line of argument, in a review of *What Is Art?* (1898), John Kenworthy, whose Brotherhood Publishing Company published the English-language edition of the book, argued that Tolstoy's work was in fact 'Ruskin systematised, simplified, clarified and proved "to the hilt."'[86] But Tolstoy went on:

> ... I've forgotten what I wrote to you about Ruskin; I'm afraid it was untrue... The main thing about Ruskin is that he could never entirely free himself from his ecclesiastical-Christian outlook. In the course of his early work on social problems when he was writing *Unto this Last* he freed himself from dogmatic tradition, but his hazy ecclesiastical-Christian understanding of the demands of life which enabled him to combine ethical

---

[82] Tolstoy, *Letters*, ed. and trans. R. F. Christian, vol. 2, p. 546.
[83] Meynell (ed.), *Friends*, p. 81.
[84] See Maude, *Problems*, pp. 40-41.
[85] Tolstoy to Maude (undated) in Tolstoy, *Letters*, ed. and trans. R. F. Christian, vol. 2, p. 600 fn. 1
[86] John Kenworthy, 'Tolstoy's "What Is Art?"' in *Saint George* vol. 1, no. 2 (April 1898) pp. 67-71, specifically p. 71. For the volume in question, see Leo Tolstoy, *What Is Art?* (London: Brotherhood Publishing Company, 1898).

> ideals with aesthetic [ones], stayed with him to the end and weakened his preaching; it was also weakened by the artificiality and hence the obscurity of his poetic language. [87]

It is still more than curious that Ruskin merited no mention at all in Tolstoy's treatise on art. But Tolstoy did not want his criticism to be misunderstood:

> Don't think that I was denigrating (*deniger*) the work of this great man who has quite rightly been called a prophet; I always admired and still admire him, but I'm indicating spots, which even the sun has. [88]

Maude added to his translation of the letter that, 'to summarise Ruskin would be perhaps more difficult than to condense Kant'![89] It is a significant comparison, because in a letter to one correspondent in 1909, Tolstoy ranked Ruskin's 'true morality' alongside Kant, Emerson, Channing, Rousseau and Pascal.[90] Tolstoy concluded a letter to Maude by remarking of Ruskin:

> He's particularly good when a clever and similarly inclined writer makes extracts from him, as in the book *Ruskin et la Bible* (Read it— but to read all Ruskin, as I did, one after another, very much weakens the effect) ... [91]

---

[87] Tolstoy to Aylmer Maude (28? July 1901) qtd in Tolstoy, *Letters*, ed. and trans. R. F. Christian, vol. 2, p. 600.
[88] Ibid., pp. 600-1.
[89] Maude, *Problem*s, p. 42.
[90] Tolstoy to Nikolay Schmidt (22 July 1909) qtd Tolstoy, *Letters*, ed. and trans. R. F. Christian, vol. 2, p. 689.
[91] Ibid., p. 601.

Whether Tolstoy remembered making the point, it was nevertheless something to which he would give active attention when, in the first decade of the twentieth century, and the final years of his life, he worked on the calendars of thoughts of wise men, in which Ruskin's words feature very strongly.

Tolstoy wrote to his friend and admirer, Gavrill Andreyevich Rusanov (1845-1907), on 24 September 1904: 'I have been busy recently compiling, not so much a calendar but a Circle of Reading for each day, compiled from the best thoughts of the best writers' and he proceeded to list Ruskin among two dozen of those from whom he quoted. It was, he implied, a project to combat 'the "cultural" barbarity in which our society is immersed'.[92]

Tolstoy collected and selected mottoes, aphorisms and maxims, —'Epigraphs of striking force' as he had called lines from Ruskin published in English-language selections—in order to compile anthologies of what he considered the wisest thoughts of the greatest thinkers: 'the cultural heritage of our ancestors, the best thinkers of the world'.[93] Collected in the course of fifteen years, *A Calendar of Wisdom* (1903-1910), the three editions of selections published under the title *Put' Zhizni* (*Path of Life*, or *Life's Way*)—with other volumes called *A Circle of Reading* and *Thoughts of Wise Men*—was Tolstoy's last major work. He explained in his introduction, written in August 1905 for the second edition, that he used a mixture of translations by himself and others, with

[92] Tolstoy to Gavrill Andreyevich Rusanov (24 September, 1904) qtd Tolstoy, *Letters*, ed. and trans. R. F. Christian, vol. 2, p. 644. (Christian notes that by 1904 Rusanov was a cripple who credited Tolstoy with his conversion to Christianity.)

[93] L. N. Tolstoy, *A Calendar of Wisdom: Wise Thoughts for Every Day*, trans. Peter Sekirin (London: Hodder & Stoughton, 1997) (1998 paperback edn) pp. viii-ix.

paraphrased and even summarised versions of the more complex arguments:

> … the purpose of my book is not to give precise, word-for-word translations of the thoughts of other authors but, using the intellectual heritage bequeathed by great writers, to present for a wide reading audience an easily accessible, everyday circle of reading that will arouse their best thoughts and feelings.
>
> I hope that readers of this book will enjoy the benign and elevating feelings which I experienced when I was working on its creation and which I experience again and again as I re-read it every day in order to enlarge and improve the text.[94]

Epictetus, Marcus Aurelius, Lao-Tzu, Pascal, Confucius, Emerson, Seneca, Jesus, Buddha, Socrates, Thoreau, Kant and Voltaire provided Ruskin with illustrious company. Svetlana Shustova wrote that, 'Tolstoy put Ruskin on a par with such philosophers as Kant. .. [and] Voltaire' and she concluded that 'Tolstoy was captivated by Ruskin's humanity and his boundless faith that people should be guided by love in all their activities.'[95]

Peter Sekirin's selective translation of Tolstoy's *Calendar* into English, contains 27 passages quoted from Ruskin (individual works are not identified), some of them short sentences, some longer excerpts. One example is taken from Letter 76 *of Fors Clavigera* (written in April 1877). (It should be remembered that this has been translated into Russian and retro-translated into English.)

---

[94] Ibid., p. vii.

[95] Shustova, 'Reskina v Rossii,' p. 200.

> We have to fulfil honestly and irreproachably the work demanded of us. And it does not matter whether we hope that we will be angels some time, or believe that we have originated from slugs.[96]

One statement he underlined from Nikiforov's three-volume *Selected Thoughts* merited quotation in his diary in 1901: '"Unless we serve God in every voluntary act of our lives we don't serve Him at all," says Ruskin. That's what one must do and remember.'[97]

Tolstoy re-read his *Calendar* every day for the last five years of his life, and he was still able to discover new meaning in Ruskin in so doing, noting in his diary in January 1906, for instance, that:

> In *The Thoughts of Wise People* today, the 6th, is Ruskin's idea that the sin of human beings is the sin of Judas, namely that people don't believe in their Christ and sell him. For the first time I understood: yes, the chief mistake —the source of all sufferings and disasters —is the fact that we don't believe in our divinity and sell it for the mess of pottage of physical joys.[98]

A wider selection from Ruskin made by Tolstoy was published in an affordable pamphlet by the popular and prolific Odessa-based publisher, M. S. Kozman, under the title *Mysli Dzhona Reskina* (*The Thoughts of John Ruskin*) in 1904.[99] In the course of 24 pages, Tolstoy reproduced 122 separate 'thoughts' from a broad range of Ruskin's work.

---

[96] Tolstoy, *Calendar*, trans. Peter Sekirin, p. 3. For Ruskin's original, see *Works* 29.88.

[97] Tolstoy, *Diaries*, ed. and trans. R. F. Christian (18 August 1901) vol. 2, p. 496.

[98] Tolstoy, *Diaries,* ed. and trans. R. F. Christian (6 January 1906) vol. 2, p. 547.

[99] Dzhon Reskin (John Ruskin), *Mysli Dzhona Reskina*, (*The Thoughts of John Ruskin*) selected by L. N. Tolstoy (Odessa: M. S. Kozman, 1904).

It must be a matter of regret that the collection has never been translated into English. Tolstoy may have despaired that the English did not appreciate Ruskin as 'a philosopher, political economist, and Christian moralist' but the same charge cannot justly be levelled at Tolstoy himself. In 2015, with the help of my notes on these maxims, Vladislava Polituciaia, a student based at Ca' Foscari University of Venice, surveyed Tolstoy's translations of Ruskin. She concluded: 'there is still a vast field to investigate in, and much information still to be discovered' but her comparison of Ruskin's original and Tolstoy's rendering of it demonstrates the promises of nuancing our understanding of Tolstoy's personal approach to Ruskin, and it is hoped that such exercises in comparative linguistics are pursued in the future.[100]

Tolstoy's selection of 122 of Ruskin 'thoughts'.

[100] See Vladislava Polituciaia, 'John Ruskin and Leo Tolstoy' supervised by Prof Emma Sdegno (unpublished thesis, Ca' Foscari University of Venice, 2015). The quoted text is on p. 19.

Ruskin on Tolstoy

What can be said of Ruskin's view of Tolstoy? W. G. Collingwood wrote in his 1893 biography of Ruskin:

> Not long since, talking over his failures, Mr Ruskin said it was some comfort to him that he was not without successors, and he instanced Count Leo Tolstoi as one who was, in a way, carrying out the work he had hoped to do.[101]

Sydney Cockerell recorded that:

> '"The Story of Count Tolstoy,"' wrote Ruskin early in 1888 to a friend who had sent him George Kennan's fine article in the *Century* for June 1887, 'is the noblest thing I ever read.' To the same friend he lamented that he had not renounced his possessions. 'If I had done this,' he said, 'and lived in a garret, I could preach that Queen Victoria should do the same. I have always held that the only way to get rid of the East End is to get rid of the West End first.' One of us quoted this remark to Tolstoy.[102] [']That interests me very much,' he said, 'for it is my case also. And why did not Ruskin do it?' 'He found it so difficult. He had so many ties, artists to support, etc.' 'Ah,' he replied with a sigh, 'that is it; we do not become Christians until late in life, and then there are ties.'[103]

Alice Meynell wrote that Ruskin 'reproached himself that he had not the courage to live in a garret or make shoes like Tolstoi (whom he

---

[101] Collingwood, *Life* (1893), vol. 2, pp. 564-5.
[102] Cockerell told his friend Blunt that he had quoted it to Tolstoy, see Blunt, *Cockerell*, p. 106.
[103] See Meynell (ed.), *Friends*, p. 82.

had not read, but heard of with sympathetic envy)'—a comment that was picked up and reproduced by Cook in his biography of Ruskin.[104]

It seems highly probable that Ruskin did not read Tolstoy. An admirer of both men, who was able to harmonise their influence to inspiration effect was John Kenworthy. He wrote that Tolstoy was 'a man whom neither Ruskin nor Morris understood. The former looked upon him, I think, as a too-distant Russian...'[105] Kenworthy was probably right in this, and it is a judgement that indicates that he was not insensitive to differences between the two men. It may seem bold to say so, given the seminal importance of these writers to such a significant figure as Mohandas Gandhi[106]—who is well served by scholars around the world, and whose influences are well understood—but Kenworthy, the leading figure in the Tolstoyan Purleigh Colony in Essex, England, who was a member and even committee man in the Liverpool Ruskin Society, and who counted among the earliest Companions of Ruskin's Guild of St

---

[104] Alice Meynell, *John Ruskin* (Edinburgh: William Blackwood and Sons, 1900), p. 272. Also, see Cook, *Life*, vol. 2, p. 563-4.

[105] John Kenworthy, *Tolstoy, His Life and Works* (London: Walter Scott, 1902) p. 12.

[106] I have written elsewhere about the complex network of mutual associations that influenced Ruskin, Tolstoy and Gandhi. In particular, Tolstoy's theory of 'bread-labour' was derived from the writings of Timofei Bondarev (1820-98), a former serf who was eventually exiled for renouncing the Orthodox Church. Tolstoy considered Ruskin's thought and Bondarev's to be similar, and he quoted *Fors Clavigera* in an essay on Bondarev published in 1897 (see *PSS*, 31.69-71; the quote from Ruskin is from *Works* 28.654). Gandhi read Tolstoy's essay and this is where he first came across *Fors* (see M. Gandhi, *The Essential Writings*, ed. Judith M. Brown (Oxford: Oxford World Classics, 2007) pp. 30-31 For a fuller account see Stuart Eagles, 'Political legacies', in Francis O'Gorman (ed.), *The Cambridge Companion to John Ruskin* (Cambridge: Cambridge University Press, 2015) pp. 249-262.

George, provides the exemplary case-study of the combined influence of Ruskin and Tolstoy.

John Coleman Kenworthy: Ruskinian and Tolstoyan

John Coleman Kenworthy

More familiar to scholars of Tolstoyism, largely by way of essays by W. H. G. Armytage and Michael Holman, Kenworthy met, wrote about, and gave practical expression to the influence of both writers.[107] Previously, scholars have made only passing reference to Kenworthy's admiration of Ruskin, neglecting entirely the evidence of his contributions to the journal of the Ruskin Society of Birmingham, *Saint George.*

The son of a master mariner, Kenworthy was born and raised in Everton, Liverpool, where he established himself as a commercial clerk and agent. When he was 20 his father died at sea, and two years later he married, in Birkenhead, the daughter of a marine engineer. He was interested in Henry George and Ralph Waldo Emerson and became a member of the socialist movement at the same time as he joined Ruskinian organisations.

Notwithstanding the fact that Kenworthy was yet to discover Tolstoy when he became a Guild Companion, it is nevertheless instructive that Tolstoy was not only aware of, but admired Ruskin's Guild. An anonymous correspondent, writing in the *Cornhill Magazine*, reported:

> I confessed to the Count that I myself only knew Ruskin as the art critic. At this he seemed much put about. 'Then,' he replied, 'you don't know anything.' I pleaded that a journalist who had to keep pace with political events of the day had little time left for studying philosophy. The Count agreed, but urged me all the same to join the Ruskin Society. [He surely meant the Guild of St George.] 'To be a member,' he said, 'you must wear nothing that has not been made by hand, nor must you live on money which has been gained by usury. You must, in a word, live by

[107] See especially W. H. G. Armytage, 'J. C. Kenworthy and the Tolstoyan Communities in England', in W. Gareth Jones (ed.), *Tolstoi in Britain*, pp. 135-152 and M. J. de K. Holman, 'The Purleigh Colony: Tolstoyan Togetherness in the late 1890s' in ibid., pp. 152-183.

your own labour, not on other people's. To many,' he added, 'these are not pleasant doctrines, few people like to be told that they are living on other people's labour.'[108]

Tolstoy's understanding of the Guild may have been imperfect, and certainly he did not seem to be aware of the difference between how the Guild operated in practice as opposed to what Ruskin wrote about it in *Fors Clavigera*, yet the fact that he thought well of the principles underlying Ruskin's project helps to explain how Kenworthy was able to combine the twin influences of the Englishman and the Russian so effortlessly.

Kenworthy never played a significant role in the Guild, sailing away from England with his young family in 1890, but he later argued that his Tolstoyan colony at Purleigh, near Maldon in the Essex hills, was as concerned with realising Ruskin's ideals as the Count's. On that theme, he spoke about 'Ruskin's Place in Our Social Movement' in 1896 to the Ruskin Society of Birmingham and received the following year a guinea from the Society towards his social work.[109] He wrote of Purleigh in *Saint George*, that 'there is in England one community at least, whose life is visibly ordered by the principles Ruskin has taught. This may be justly said of the group at Purleigh ... .'[110] He concluded: 'It may be said that John Ruskin's criticism of existing social and economic conditions is taken for granted in the thought of the colony.'[111] Of course the fact

---

[108] Anon., 'A Visit to Count Tolstoi,' in *Cornhill Magazine*, series 2, vol. 18, no. 108 (June 1892) pp. 597-610, specifically p. 605.

[109] Ruskin Library: Ruskin Society of Birmingham Minute Book (12 March 1897). The lecture took place on 11 November 1896.

[110] John Kenworthy, 'The Purleigh Colony' in *Saint George*, vol. 1, no. 4 (October 1898) pp. 202-7, specifically p. 202.

[111] Ibid., p. 204. Richard J. Hine, letter of response to Kenworthy (29 October 1898) *Saint George* vol. 2, no. 5 (January 1899) pp. 42-45. Hine wrote, he explained,'not in any spirit of personal criticism' (p. 42) wishing the Purleigh

that such testimony is recorded in a Ruskin Society journal necessarily prejudices it as evidence, but there is no reason to doubt Kenworthy's sincerity.

Colony House, Purleigh:
vestiges of utopia survive in the 21st century.

It was in his adopted country, America, that Kenworthy discovered the works of Tolstoy, and as he later wrote in *Saint George*, he 'found in [Tolstoy's] writings ... the confirmation and expansion of all I had thought and felt.'[112] Returning to England in July 1892, he immersed himself in the problems of the poor, working with various co-operative ventures in Canning Town linked to the Mansfield House

colonists all the best, but expressed considerable skepticism about the scheme..

[112] Kenworthy, 'Purleigh Colony', p. 205.

University Settlement. He became the central figure of the Croydon Brotherhood Church, established a press which went on to publish many of Tolstoy's works translated into English. He even travelled to Yasnaya Polyana and met Tolstoy himself.

Tolstoy liked him on a personal level: 'It's two days since Kenworthy arrived,' he wrote in his diary. 'He's very pleasant.'[113] Kenworthy was a prolific writer, and Tolstoy appreciated his books and owned at least ten volumes written by him.[114] It ought to be recognised, however, that Tolstoy's literary tastes were not merely idiosyncratic, but sometimes eccentric in the extreme. He once told Chekhov, 'I can't stand your plays. Shakespeare wrote badly, and you're even worse!'[115] Cockerell quoted Tolstoy as saying, 'I have read Shakespeare, but I never liked him .. Shakespeare had no feeling for the peasants. He never introduces a "clown" except to make fun of him. This is why I cannot read him with pleasure.'[116] Another visitor recalled Tolstoy 'speaking in the same breath and with equal persuasion of Ruskin, Dickens and J. Morrison's *Annals of the Poor*, which he regarded as a masterpiece.'[117]

---

[113] Tolstoy, *Diaries*, ed. and trans. R. F. Christian (23 December 1895) vol. 2, p. 421.
[114] See Tolstoy on Kenworthy in Tolstoy, *Diaries*, ed. and trans. R. F. Christian (15 May 1894) vol. 1, p. 332. On his Kenworthy collection, see Bulgakov, Gusev and Novikova (eds), *Biblioteka L'va Nikolaevicha Tolstogo*, items 1756-1765.
[115] Qtd in I. A. Bunin, *Sobranie sochinenii* (*Collected Works*) (9 vols.) (Moscow, 1967) vol. 9, p. 207.
[116] See Meynell (ed.), *Friends*, pp. 83-4. Cockerell wrote to Blunt that, 'This struck me as a very just criticism,' see Blunt, *Cockerell*, p. 106.
[117] Charles Sarolea (1870-1953), a Belgian who occupied the Chair of French at Edinburgh University, recalling a conversation with Tolstoy which probably took place in 1908. R. F. Christian, 'The Road to Yasnaya Polyana: Some Pilgrims from Britain and Their Reminiscences' in W. Gareth Jones (ed.) *Tolstoi and Britain* (Oxford: Berg, 1995) pp.185-216, specifically p. 210.

Kenworthy's *The Anatomy of Misery* (1893) presents a competent and persuasive social and politico-economic analysis in the Ruskin-Tolstoy tradition, but it was as undeserving of the highest praise as Shakespeare was of censure. Tolstoy caused it to be translated into Russian, and in a preface to its second edition in English, he wrote, after praising its brevity, that it contained 'more solid matter' than much longer works:

> ... it states economic problems clearly and simply. Anyone who reads this book with unprejudiced mind and sincere desire to find answers to the problems which confront people of our times, will find those answers, and will arrive at a clear understanding of things which most people imagine to be difficult and obstruse (sic). He will find also moral guidance and stimulation to good.
>
> We should all like our social arrangements better ordered than they are now. To move in this direction we must ourselves become better. It is the only way. There is no other.
>
> It is this simple truth which, however, we always forget, that is with clearness and convincing power, set forth by the present work.[118]

Kenworthy invoked Ruskin alongside Owen and Marx in his analysis in order to contrast them with Smith, Ricardo and (less convincingly) John Stuart Mill. The priority of the first group, he argued, was always 'Moral' since for them 'Happiness, development, [and]

---

[118] Tolstoy's introduction to John Coleman Kenworthy, *The Anatomy of Misery*: *Plain Lectures on Economics* (2nd edn) (London: John C. Kenworthy, 1900) p. 13, (introduction written at Yasnaya Polyana on 2 June 1900).

pleasurable activity' is 'the purpose of human life'.[119] Resurrecting the true meaning of the Biblical instruction, 'Thou shalt love thy neighbour as thyself,' Kenworthy emphasised the paramountcy of mutual interdependence in an 'organic' community.[120]

It is in the context of the ideal community that Kenworthy and his friends established at Purleigh, that his fusion of Ruskinian and Tolstoyan values was most clearly articulated. Tolstoy's idolisation of the peasant may not be difficult to reconcile with Ruskin's less exaggerated respect for the labourer in the field, but a community based on Tolstoyan anarcho-communist principles might seem to be anathema to Ruskinian values of order and hierarchy. The Russian context of Tolstoy's advocacy of communism might suggest otherwise, however, and contemporaries were perhaps better placed to recognise an affinity here than we are. Having visited Yasnaya Polyana, the journalist W. T. Stead (1849-1912), in his book, *Truth About Russia* (1888) wrote:

> on the whole, it is not only Mr. Ruskin who would say that the life of a Russian peasant is more natural and human, and therefore has greater opportunities for attaining to the ideal and the divine than the life of a resident in our London slums.[121]

Stead was not alone in making a connection between Ruskin, the Russian peasant and communal life. The journalist, Stephen Graham (1884-1975), who contributed so significantly to the British understanding of Russian life in the early twentieth century, recognised the Ruskinian spirit of the Russian peasantry. The language now seems patronising, and some of the judgements have been overtaken and

---

[119] Ibid., p. 24.
[120] Ibid., p. 25.
[121] W. T. Stead, *Truth About Russia* (London: Cassell, 1888) p. 186.

undermined by subsequent events, but his observations are significant. In the preface to his book, *Undiscovered Russia* (1912), Graham wrote:

> The Russians are an agricultural nation, bred to the soil, illiterate as the savages, and having as yet no ambition to live in the towns. They are strong as giants, simple as children, mystically superstitious by reason of their unexplained mystery. They live as Ruskin wished the English to live, some of them, as he tried to persuade the English to live by his "Fors Clavigera". They are obediently religious, seriously respectful to their elders, true to the soil they plough, content with the old implements of culture, not using machinery or machine-made things, but able themselves to fashion out of the pine all that they need. But they have all the while been doing this, and have never fallen away as the English have. There is no 'back to the land' problem in Russia, nor will there be for a hundred years.
>
> The Liberal press and the revolutionaries would like to educate the peasantry to give them a vote. They would at the same time place no restraints on Russian manufacture and the freedom of town life, and so once more betray the country to the town and rush into all the errors of Western Europe. England has fallen away from the soil and ceased to produce its own food, and not Ruskin, nor all the king's horses and all the king's men could replace her where she was. [122]

---

[122] Stephen Graham, *Undiscovered Russia* (London: John Lane, 1912) pp. ix-x. Cockerell recognised the same connection, see Meynell (ed.), *Friends*, p. 84 and Blunt, *Cockerell*, p. 106.

The Russian critic and writer, Konstantin Aksakov (1817-1860), wrote an influential description of the Russian commune which is not difficult to reconcile to Ruskinian and Tolstoyan priorities, and it describes what Kenworthy and his colonists were seeking after in their English experiment:

> A commune is a union of the people who have renounced their egoism, their individuality, and who express their common accord; this is an act of love, a noble Christian act, which expresses itself more or less clearly in its various other manifestations. A commune thus represents a moral choir, and just as in a choir a voice is not lost, but follows the general pattern and is heard in the harmony of all voices; so in the commune the individual is not lost, but renounces his exclusiveness in favour of a general accord – and there arises the noble phenomenon of a harmonious, joint existence of rational beings (consciousness); there arises a brotherhood, a commune – a triumph of the human spirit.[123]

The Purleigh Colony was short-lived, and scholars have already more than adequately explained how a mixture of financial difficulty, unresolved organisational dispute and personal disagreement and rivalry combined to cause its collapse. It even contributed to the deterioration of Kenworthy's mental health.

Ultimately, it should be remembered that Tolstoy was not a good Tolstoyan, and Ruskin was not a good Ruskinian. Neither of them wanted to be, nor for that matter, did they wish anybody else to waste time in an attempt to embody their philosophies whole. Disciples were not

---

[123] Konstantin Aksakov, 'Brief Sketch of the Zemskie Sobory,' *Sochineniya istoricheskie* (*Historical Essays*) (Moscow, 1861) pp. 291-2.

infrequently disappointed to discover their heroes falling short of their own standards. W. T. Stead wrote:

> During my week's sojourn at Yasnaia Poliana, the Count did no manual toil. He had not made any shoes for some time, and although he proposed ploughing the field of a peasant woman whose husband was in gaol for horse-stealing, he did not actually get between the stilts.[124]

Yet the disciples continued to admire their masters. 'A Ruskin, a Tolstoy, great seer, great teacher,' Kenworthy wrote, 'lives and works by and for his conception of life. It is his beginning and his end. His earliest utterances prophesy the revelation of it; his later, exhibit it, and expand it.'[125]

* * *

For enthusiasts such as Kenworthy, drawn to listen to the prophetic voices in the world, Tolstoy and Ruskin, whatever the differences between their views on this matter or that—differences which ultimately they dismissed as superficial and unimportant—were connected at a fundamental level. Theirs was a shared spirit.

> The writer who most resembles Tolstoy in his general attitude of mind, great range of feeling, thought, and knowledge, and in his intense vitality, is our English Ruskin. In distinguishing the two, one would, I think, ascribe to Ruskin, fineness; to Tolstoy, robustness. But

---

[124] Stead, Truth About Russia, p. 402-3. He does go on, however, 'He really did not seem to have sufficient physical strength to do a long day's hard work' (p. 403).

[125] Kenworthy, 'Tolstoy's "What Is Art?"' in *Saint George*, vol. 1, no. 2 (April 1898) p. 68.

> their general harmony is complete: both are world-prophets.[126]

When Edward Bernstein, author and Tolstoy enthusiast, heard in December 1941 that German troops were devastating the city of Tula and were threatening to capture Yasnaya Polyana nearby, he wrote to *The Times*, 'one trusts that whatever still remains of Tolstoy's house and estate will be taken greater care of, so that the memory and influence of that great mind and spirit may be more widely felt and more perfectly esteemed.' Recalling his experience of the Tolstoy centenary celebrations of 1928, he remembered that next to Tolstoy's bedroom was:

> the pleasant little library in which he sat and studied. It was in that room that he sat reading before he left his home on his final journey, one early, dark October morning, in the company of his daughter Alexandra. The room had been jealously preserved, just as he left it, with some of the books, among them works by Ruskin and Carlyle, open at the page which he had been reading.[127]

On another anniversary, Tolstoy's 80th birthday in 1908, many of his disciples were keen to celebrate his life and achievements, but Tolstoy could muster no personal enthusiasm for the idea, nevertheless conceding in a letter to Vladimir Chertkov, '... if, for instance, Ruskin or Dickens were still alive, and it was a question of expressing one's sympathy for them, I would feel the desire to participate.'[128]

Tolstoy wrote in 1903 to Percy Redfern (1875-1958), later the leading historian of the co-operative movement, but then secretary of the

---

[126] Kenworthy, *Tolstoy*, p. 36.
[127] Edward Bernstein, 'Letters,' in *The Times* (27 December 1941), p. 5.
[128] Tolstoy to Chertkov qtd Vladimir Chertkov, 'Tolstoy Jubilee', 'Letters,' *The Times* (21 May 1908), p. 16.

Manchester Tolstoy Society, founded in 1900: 'Ruskin says that the best men, those which have done the greatest good to humanity, are those that we do not know of.'[129] In his biography of Ruskin, Collingwood quotes from a source which endorses this view. In ending with it, let the words stand as an assessment of the degree of influence achieved by both men since their deaths, and let there be no doubt that Tolstoy knew Ruskin's work well and profoundly respected his work and ideas.

> Last June, in the 'Cornhill Magazine,' in which *Unto This Last* appeared over thirty years ago, a contributor reported his talk with the great Russian: 'Ruskin he thought one of the greatest men of the age; and it pained him to notice that English people generally were of a different opinion. But no man is a prophet in his own country, and the greatest men are seldom recognized in their own times, for the very reason that they are so much in advance of the age. Their contemporaries are unable to understand them."[130]
>
> So Tolstoi speaks, so all the best men of his time have spoken about Ruskin; and after theirs, what testimony can be added?[131]

---

[129] Tolstoy to Percy Redfern (23 February 1903) in Tolstoy, *Letters*, ed. and trans. R. F. Christian, vol. 2, p. 630.

[130] Anon., 'Visit,' in *Cornhill*, p. 605. The anonymous correspondent is the same source quoted from the *Pall Mall Gazette* by Cook and Wedderburn (quoted above).

[131] Collingwood, *Life* (1893) vol. 2, pp. 564-5.

SELECT BIBLIOGRAPHY

Ruskin-related material in Russian

(a) Translations of Ruskin by Lev Pavlovich Nikiforov (1848-1917) [in date order]

Reskin, Dzhon (Ruskin, John), *Tsar' Zolotoi Reki ili "Chernye Brat'ya": (Shtiriisk. Legenda Dzhona Reskina)* (*The King of the Golden River, or "The Black Brothers" (Styrian. Legend by John Ruskin)*) (Moscow: P. K. Pryanishnikov, 1894) (reissued: 1, Moscow: Vil'de, 1901; 2, Moscow: Posrednik, 1903; 3, Moscow: Posrednik, 1910; 4, St Petersburg: A. F. Sukhov, 1912).

—, *Vospitanie. Kniga. Zhenshchina* (*Education. Book. Woman*) (Moscow: I. A. Balandin, 1898) (preface by Lev Nikolaevich Tolstoi) (reissued, 1901).

—, *Izbrannye Mysli Dzhona Reskina* (*The Selected Thoughts of John Ruskin*) (3 vols.) (Moscow: Posrednik, 1899, 1902, 1904) (reissued: Moscow: Vil'de, 1912).

—, *Sobranie Sochinenii/Sochineniya Dzhona Reski*na (*The Collected Works/The Works of John Ruskin*) series 1 (10 vols.) series 2 (1 vol.) (1900-1905).

series 1, vol. 1, *Sesam i Lilii* (*Sesame and Lilies*) (Moscow: I. A. Balandin, 1900).

series 1, vol. 2, *Pis'ma i sovety zhenshinam molodym devukam* (*Letters and Advice to Women and Young Girls*) (Moscow: I. A. Balandin, 1900).

series 1, vol. 3, *Poslednemu, chto i pervomu: chetyre ocherka osnov printsipov politecheskoi ékonomii* (i.e. *Unto this Last* [literally, *The Latter, as the First]*: *four essays on the principles of political economy*) (Moscow: I. A. Balandin, 1900) (reissued: 1, Moscow: Posrednik, 1906 – with subtitle changed to *ocherki po rabochemu voprosu* (*essays on the labour question*); 2, Moscow: Posrednik, 1910).

series 1, vol. 4, *Lektsii ob iskussstve, chitannye v Oksfordskom universitete v 1870 godu* (*Lectures on Art, delivered at Oxford University in 1870*) (Moscow: I. A. Balandin, 1900).

series 1, vol. 5, *Olivkovyi venok: chetyre lektsii o promyshlennosti i voine* (*The Crown of Wild Olive: four lectures on industry and war*) (Moscow: I. A. Balandin, 1900).

series 1, vol. 6, *Étika pyli* (*Ethics of the Dust*) (Moscow: V. N. Lind and I. A. Balandin, 1901).

series 1, vol. 7, *Sel'skie list'ya: Otryvki iz "Sovremennykh zhivopistsev"* (*Rural Leaves: Excerpts from "Modern Painters"* [i.e. *Frondes Argrestes*]) (Moscow: V. N. Lind and I. A. Balandin, 1902).

series 1, vol. 8, *Radost' navek i ee rynichnaya tsena, ili Politicheskaya ékonomiya iskusstva* (*A Joy For Ever, and its Market Price, or the Political Economy of Art*) (Moscow: V. N. Lind and I. A. Balandin, 1902) (reissued, Moscow: Komkniga*, 2007).

series 1, vol. 9, *Zakony Fiesolo* (*Laws of Fesole*) (Moscow: Knizhnoe Delo, 1904) (reissued, Moscow: Komkniga*, 2007).

series 1, vol. 10, *Orlinoe Gnesdo: 10 lektsii ob otnoshenii estestvoznaniya k iskusstvu* (*The Eagle's Nest: 10 lectures on the relation of natural science to art*) (Moscow: Knizhnoe Delo, 1903).

series 2, vol. 1, *Fors Klavidzhera*, *Pis'ma k rabochim i zemledel'tsam Velikobritanii* (*Fors Clavigera, Letters to the Workers and Farmers of Great Britain*) (Moscow: Knizhnoe Delo, 1905).

*issued in Komkniga's series *Iz naslediya mirovoi filosofskoi mysli. Estetika* (*World Heritage of Philosophical Thought. Aesthetics*).

(b) Other Ruskin-related translations cited in the text

Brunges, G. I. (Bruhnès, H. I.), *Reskin i Bibliya: k istorii odnoi mysli* (*Ruskin and the Bible: A History of His Thought*) trans. L. P. Nikiforov [vol. 90 in the series (for Intelligent Readers)] (Moscow: Posrednik, 1901) [i.e. Henrietta Bruhnès, *Ruskin et la Bible: pour servir a l'histoire d'une pensée* (Paris: Perrin, 1901)].

Gobson, Dzhon (John Hobson), *Dzhon Rëskin, kak sotsial'nyi reformator* (*John Ruskin as a Social Reformer*) trans. L. P. Nikiforov (Moscow: K. T. Soldatenkov, 1899) [i.e. J. A. Hobson, *John Ruskin, Social Reformer* (London: Nisbet, 1898)].

Reskin, Dzhon, *Iskusstvo i* deistvitel'nost': izbrannye stranitsy (*Art and Reality: Selected Passages*) ed. and trans. Olga Solov'eva (Moscow: 1, I. N. Kushnerev, 1900; 2. A. I. Mamontov, 1900).

Reskin, Dzhon (Ruskin, John), *Mysli Dzhona Reskina* (*The Thoughts of John Ruskin*) trans. and selected by L. N. Tolstoy (Odessa: M. S. Kozman, 1904).

Ol'den-Uard, M. (Ward, May Alden),*Tri Biografii: Tomas Karleil', Dzhon Reskin, Lev Tolstoi* (*Three Biographies: Thomas Carlyle, John Ruskin, Lev Tolstoi*) trans. I. S. Durnovo (Moscow: M. V. Klyukin, 1900) [i.e. May Alden Ward, *Prophets of the Nineteenth Century: Carlyle, Ruskin, Tolstoi* (London: Gay and Bird, 1900)].

Sizerann, Robert (la Sizeranne, Robert de), *Reskin i religiya krasoty* (*Ruskin and the Religion of Beauty*) trans. L. P. Nikiforov (Moscow: Magazina "Knizhnoe Delo" and I. A. Balandin, 1900) (reissued, Moscow: Komkniga*, 2007) [i.e. Robert de la Sizeranne, *Ruskin et la religion de la beauté* (Paris, 1897)].

(c) Studies of Ruskin in Russian cited in the text

Nikiforov, Lev Pavlovich, *Dzhon Reskin. Ego zhizn', idei i deyatel'nost', Biograficheskii ocherk* (*John Ruskin. His Life, Ideas and Work, A Biographical Sketch*) [*s portretom Reskina* (*with a portrait of Ruskin)*] ['Wise Men' series (issue 57)] (Moscow: Posrednik, 1896).

Nikitina, T. V., 'Dialog drukh kul'tur: Lev Tolstoi i Dzhon Reskin' ('A Dialogue Between Two Cultures: Lev Tolstoy and John Ruskin'), in *Yasnopolyanskii Sbornik* (*Yasnaya Polyana: A Collection*) (Tula: Yasnaya Polyana Publishing House, 2000), pp. 274-278.

Shustova, S. R., 'K voprosu o roli L. N. Tolstogo v rasporstranenii trudov Dzhona Reskina v Rossii' ('The role of L. N. Tolstoy in disseminating the work of John Ruskin in Russia) in *Problemy fol'kloristiki, istorii, literatury i metodiki ee preobodavaniya* (*Problems of Folklore: The History of Literature and its Teaching*) (Kyibyshev, 1972) pp. 199-201.

Other Publications from the Guild of St George

The Ruskin Lecture: Original Series

1978 Lord Asa Briggs
1979 Robert Hewison: Art & Society. Ruskin in Sheffield in 1876
1981 Philip Rawson: Ruskin, Turner and Time
1982 Van Akin Burd: Ruskin, Lady Mount Temple and the Spiritualists
1982 Michael Kitson: Ruskin's 'Stones of Venice'
1983 Joe Holyoak: J. H. Chamberlain. Ruskin's architect of the Civic Gospel
1985 Anthony Harris: Why do our little girls have large shoes?
1986 Tim Hilton: Ruskin's Masterpiece
1987 Sir Roy Shaw: The Relevance of Ruskin
1988 Nicholas Shrimpton: Ruskin and 'War' [published 2014]
1991 Anthony Harris: Ruskin and Siena
1992 Malcolm Cole: Be like Daisies
1994 Royal W. Leith III: Ruskin and his American followers in Tuscany

The Ruskin Lecture: New Series

2005 Stephen Wildman: Thomas Matthews Rooke [published 2013]
2006 Sam Smiles: Ruskin and Cambridge
2007 Jacqueline Yallop: Our Power to Bequeath
2008 Paul Tucker: Charles Fairfax Murray and Duccio's *Maesta*
2009 Robert Hewison: Of Ruskin's Gardens
2010 Stuart Eagles: Ruskin and Tolstoy
2011 Zoe Bennett: The True Use of Faith
2012 Howard Hull: Demeter's Dowry: Ruskin and Landscape
2013 Mark Frost: Curator and Curatress: The Swans and St George's Museum
2014 Gray Brechin: 'Necessitous Men Are Not Free Men': Bridging Ruskin's Thought and the New Deal
2015 Marcus Waithe, Ruskin and Craftsmanship

Whitelands Ruskin Lecture

2014 Dinah Birch: Thinking Through the Past: John Ruskin and the Whitelands College May Festival
2015 Sara Atwood: 'An enormous difference between knowledge and education': What Ruskin Can Teach Us
2016 Rachel Dickinson: 'What do you mean by dressing?': Ruskin and Dress

Occasional Lectures and Other Publications

2007 Peter Wardle and Cedric Quayle: Ruskin and Bewdley
2010 James S. Dearden: John Ruskin's Guild of St George

2013 James S. Dearden (ed.): The Roll of Companions of the Guild of St George

2014 Clive Wilmer: 'A new road on which the world should travel': John Ruskin, 'The Nature of Gothic' and William Morris (William Morris Birthday Lecture)

2015 Sara Atwood: 'The earth-veil': Ruskin and Environment (A lecture given at Brantwood)

2015 Stuart Eagles: Miss Margaret E. Knight and St George's Field, Sheepscombe

2015 Annie Creswick Dawson with Paul Dawson: Benjamin Creswick

The Guild also publishes a wide selection of greetings and Christmas cards based on artworks in the Ruskin Collection.

www.guildofstgeorge.org.uk/shop
Email: publications@guildofstgeorge.org.uk

Reviews of the First Edition

'It is among the most original and thought-provoking empirical studies of Ruskin I have read, and, with *After Ruskin*, helps to establish Eagles as the leading authority on Ruskin's reception.'

—Francis O' Gorman,
Saintsbury Professor of English Literature, University of Edinburgh.

'Stuart Eagles ... has substantially extended the boundaries of what we know about Ruskin's influence, not only on Tolstoy, but also in Russia in general. The link between Ruskin and Tolstoy has often been commented on of course, but here in this essay the details and substance of that connection are fully articulated for the first time.'

—Alan Davis,
Honorary Visiting Fellow, Ruskin Library and Research Centre.
University of Lancaster.

'This is a very important, impressive and significant work.'

—Tatiana Nikitina,
Senior Researcher, Yasnaya Polyana.

'… full of insight and measured commentary ... a combination of detailed and persistent archival research and incisive critical analysis ... Having shone in a light into a little-explored area of Ruskin's work and influence, he left me, for one, hoping for more in future ...'

—Mark Frost,
Senior Lecturer in English Literature, University of Portsmouth.

'*Ruskin and Tolstoy* [is] full of fascinating detail ... it reminded me just how important the English authors were to the development of Russian culture in the nineteenth century. But ... so used to looking at everything through British spectacles (Tolstoyanism in Britain rather than Ruskinism in Russia as it were) ... reading a piece like [this] produces a very strong effect of defamiliarisation.'

—Anna Vaninskaya,
Senior Lecturer in English Literature, University of Edinburgh.

"… really enjoyable... and very useful"

—Charlotte Alston,
Reader in History, Northumbria University,
& author, *Tolstoy and His Disciples*.

'… absolutely fascinating — what an incredibly rigorously researched piece.'

—Rebecca Beasley,
Associate Professor and Tutorial Fellow in English,
The Queen's College, University of Oxford
& Co-Founder, Anglo-Russian Research Network.

'[an] excellent pamphlet, *Ruskin and Tolstoy* is very nicely put together.'

—Michael J. de K. Holman,
Professor Emeritus of Russian Studies, University of Leeds.

The Guild of St George was formally established by John Ruskin in 1878. Through the Guild, Ruskin strove to make Britain a pleasanter and happier place in which to live. His aims and aspirations for the Guild are contained in the ninety six letters of his *Fors Clavigera*. Today the Guild is a charitable Education Trust which tries to put Ruskin's ideas into practice. Its activities are reported in its annual magazine, *The Companion*, social media and its website.

The Guild owns and supports the Ruskin Collection, displayed in Sheffield's Millennium Gallery. It is running an ongoing series of activities and events in a community heritage project, *Ruskin-in-Sheffield*. Three Ruskin Triennial Exhibitions at the Millennium Gallery were initiated and sponsored by the Guild. Works from the Ruskin Collection, loans from other institutions and new commissions were exhibited to explore Ruskin's ideas in relation to issues and themes of contemporary concern: the Environment and Sustainability, Landscape and Creativity, and Craftsmanship. In 2000, it launched the Campaign for Drawing, now an independent charity called the Big Draw, which runs the Guild's John Ruskin Prize to stimulate and promote contemporary artists.

The Guild is also supporting work on the sustainable development of the Wyre Forest, where it owns farmland and 100 acres of woodland. It is regenerating old orchards and hay meadows, renovating and improving its properties, and exploring new projects and programmes of activity. It owns arts-and-crafts houses in Westmill, Hertfordshire, and is custodian of a wildflower meadow in Sheepscombe, Gloucestershire, preserved for the enjoyment of local residents and visitors.

A series of symposia held in London have considered the environment, the economy and craftsmanship from a Ruskinian view-point. The annual Ruskin Lecture, and Whitelands Ruskin Lecture, which the Guild also publishes, cover a wide range of topics of interest to Ruskin and Ruskinians. The present volume is a second edition of the Ruskin Lecture given by Stuart Eagles in November 2010 to mark the centenary of the death of Leo Tolstoy.